A BUSES MAGAZINE SPECIAL PUBLICATION

CONTENTS

BELOW: Also uniting arms of state ownership is this 1984 view of NBC's National Holidays branding on MPE371 (GLS 951V), a Duple Dominant-bodied Leyland Leopard in SBG's Alexander (Midland) fleet. GAVIN BOOTH

Senior editor, specials: Roger Mortimer
Email: roger.mortimer@keypublishing.com
Design: SJmagic DESIGN SERVICES, India
Cover: Dan Jarman
Advertising Sales Manager: Brodie Baxter
Email: brodie.baxter@keypublishing.com
Tel: 01780 755131
Advertising Production: Debi McGowan
Email: debi.mcgowan@keypublishing.com

SUBSCRIPTION/MAIL ORDER
Key Publishing Ltd, PO Box 300, Stamford, Lincs, PE9 1NA
Tel: 01780 480404
Subscriptions email: subs@keypublishing.com
Mail Order email: orders@keypublishing.com
Website: www.keypublishing.com/shop

PUBLISHING
Group CEO: Adrian Cox
Publisher, Books and Bookazines: Jonathan Jackson
Head of Marketing: Shaun Binnington
Published by
Key Publishing Ltd, PO Box 100, Stamford, Lincs, PE9 1XQ
Tel: 01780 755131
Website: www.keypublishing.com

PRINTING
Precision Colour Printing Ltd, Haldane, Halesfield 1, Telford, Shropshire. TF7 4QQ

DISTRIBUTION
Seymour Distribution Ltd, 2 Poultry Avenue, London, EC1A 9PU
Enquiries Line: 02074 294000.

We are unable to guarantee the bonafides of any of our advertisers. Readers are strongly recommended to take their own precautions before parting with any information or item of value, including, but not limited to money, manuscripts, photographs, or personal information in response to any advertisements within this publication.

© Key Publishing Ltd 2022 All rights reserved. No part of this magazine may be reproduced or transmitted in any form by any means, electronic or mechanical, including photocopying, recording or by any information storage and retrieval system, without prior permission in writing from the copyright owner. Multiple copying of the contents of the magazine without prior written approval is not permitted.

COVER: Spanning two of the major state-owned operating groups is now preserved Eastern Counties VR303 (LFS 303F), an ECW-bodied Bristol VRTLL that started was new in 1968 as Eastern Scottish AA303 and was part of the exchange of Scottish Bus Group VRTs for National Bus Company Bristol Lodekkas. JULIAN PATTERSON

The train connection

ALAN MILLAR sets the scene by explaining the railway connection behind the fact that much of the bus industry in the UK had come into state ownership by 1969 and how all but one important part of it was privatised between 1986 and 1994

Substantial parts of the British bus industry were in state ownership from the late 1940s to the early 1990s. Out of 70,000 buses and coaches licensed in England, Wales and Scotland in 1984, just before a process of privatisation got under way, 24,400 were state-owned by the National Bus Company, Scottish Bus Group and London Regional Transport.

That was more than one out of every three vehicles, spread across most parts of the British mainland and a handful of islands. This was part of a bigger picture of public ownership, as local authorities and the passenger transport executives in the seven largest city regions

outside London owned over 15,000 other buses. Add the two sectors together and 56% of all vehicles were owned either by the state or local authorities and executives.

Only a small proportion of the remaining 30,500 provided public bus services — the exceptions were mainly very long established private businesses that held road service licences in a few urban areas — notably Co. Durham, Nottinghamshire and Derbyshire, south Lincolnshire, Ayrshire and Renfrewshire — and coach operators serving deeply rural areas that the large state-owned companies were happy to leave alone or might even have abandoned.

Barely registering among those small independents in 1984 was

a four-year-old family-owned operator in Perthshire that called itself Stagecoach; it had taken advantage of legislation that abolished the need to apply for road service licences for express services and was becoming well known in parts of Scotland. Within three years, it would start buying state-owned bus companies as the government of the day put them up for sale and would own many more of them 20 years later. Its story, however, is for another day. This is the one about how the state became involved in running so many of Britain's buses and how they were organised.

It starts with railways. The rise of road transport after World War One — driven by technical advances in vehicle design to meet the needs of the military, and the release of vehicle-savvy ex-service personnel into civilian life when the four-year conflict ended — broke the virtual monopoly that the railways had enjoyed for decades in transporting people and goods. Buses and lorries provided transport that was often cheaper, quicker and more direct. The railways were rattled as business ebbed away and in 1928 they secured powers to operate their own bus services.

The Great Western Railway (GWR) and London & North Eastern Railway (LNER) already operated buses in a few areas, but rather than expand their direct operations, together with the London Midland & Scottish (LMS) and Southern Railway, they embarked on a policy of acquiring a shareholding — usually 50% — in the regional bus companies that were taking shape across England, Wales and Scotland.

Most of these were owned either by Thomas Tilling, a business with origins as an operator of horse buses in London, British Electric Traction which had diversified from electric trams in mainly urban areas and expanded into motorbuses, and Scottish Motor Traction (SMT). Some companies were owned jointly by BET and Tilling in a joint venture called Tilling & British Automobile Traction, which was broken up in 1942.

The GWR and LNER bus services were transferred to

companies in which the railways had acquired a shareholding. The Western National and Western Welsh companies were so named because the GWR part-owned them; likewise Southern National and Southern Vectis which had a Southern Railway shareholding.

The railways distanced themselves from day-to-day management of the bus companies, but were happy to close loss-making branch lines and stations in areas where railway-owned bus companies could provide often more frequent replacement services and turn in a profit for good measure. Some tickets became inter-available on buses and trains.

The Tilling & BAT alliance ended at a time when public ownership was already being mooted for postwar Britain. Tilling was receptive towards the idea, while BET was not. And once a Labour government was

elected in 1945 with a manifesto commitment to nationalise or otherwise take large parts of the economy into state ownership, that split of opinion would determine how, when and where the bus industry left the private sector.

British Transport Commission
Legislation passed in 1947 paved the way for what was to happen, starting with the nationalisation of the four main line railway companies — which had been in government control for the duration of World War Two — and their transfer to the newly created British Railways in January 1948. The railway companies' shareholdings in the Tilling, BET and SMT companies passed to British Railways, as did railway shares in municipal bus operations in Sheffield, Huddersfield, Halifax and Todmorden in Yorkshire, but we

LEFT: Railway ownership of bus companies was not usually declared in public, but the initials of both the Great Western Railway and the Southern Railway were on the side of Southern National 239 (ETA 986), a Beadle-bodied Bristol GO5G new in 1937. It was operating a Weymouth area route that incorporated the last railway-operated bus service in Britain, the GWR's Radipole route which Southern National took over in January 1934. The Southern in the bus company's name acknowledged that the Southern Railway had a shareholding. DWK JONES

BELOW: Typical of SMT group vehicles was P533 (WG 8112) in the Alexander fleet, a 1939 Leyland Tiger TS8 with 35-seat body built by Alexander's coachbuilding department in Stirling. When photographed 23 years later in Dundee, it had survived long enough to be in the Alexander (Northern) fleet formed the previous year out of the old company's Northern area. IAIN MacGREGOR

RIGHT: Although they retained their traditional liveries, the former Balfour Beatty companies in the East Midlands bought Tilling group standard vehicles once they came into state ownership. This is Notts & Derby 301 (SRB 529), a 1954 Bristol KSW6G with highbridge ECW body, in Nottingham in September 1963.
IAIN MacGREGOR

BELOW: The revolutionary ECW-bodied Bristol Lodekka, the first lowheight double-decker to go into production with the centre gangway layout of highbridge vehicles, was developed just as state ownership confined the manufacturers to supplying state-owned fleets. It became the standard double-decker for the Tilling fleets in England and Wales, and also met a substantial part of the Scottish operators' needs. Thames Valley 779 (NBL 736) was one of the first 30ft long 70-seat versions, an LDL6G new in 1957.
IAIN MacGREGOR

need to wait a little longer to pick up that part of the story.

British Railways was but part of something bigger, a multi-modal organisation named the British Transport Commission (BTC) which was to oversee railways, buses, canals, coastal shipping, road haulage and various activities like hotels and the Thomas Cook travel agency which were taken over along with the railways that owned them.

BTC began life on the same day as British Railways and also took over London Transport which since its formation in 1933 had been an autonomous public board (also in government control in the war years). Its blueprint for public transport outside London was to replicate London Transport around the land, with area boards acquiring all company and municipal buses, trolleybuses and trams, an ambition never realised

largely because of a change of government in 1951, but also through resistance from local authorities, many of them Labour-controlled.

BTC's first move into running buses outside London was in the East Midlands as a consequence of another part of the nationalisation programme. The British Electricity Authority was taking over power distribution and in April 1948 acquired

the Midland Counties Electric Supply Company from Balfour Beatty, a company that became better known for its interests in construction. Balfour Beatty had invested in tramways and Midland Counties owned three companies by then running trolleybuses and motorbuses — Mansfield District, Midland General and Notts & Derby. The three companies were transferred immediately to BTC which was preparing to fry much larger fish.

In September 1948, Tilling agreed the sale to BTC of its bus companies in England, Wales and south-west Scotland for £24.8million, which at 2021 values is about £630million. SMT followed suit in April 1949, securing a £26.8million price for a substantially smaller business than Tilling's, one worth around £650million today. That deal was backdated to April 1948 and SMT's operations became known initially as the BTC's Scottish Omnibuses group, later informally and then formally as Scottish Bus Group (SBG).

Tilling and SMT were also involved in bus manufacturing. Tilling owned Eastern Coach Works (ECW) at Lowestoft, which built may of the group's bus and coach bodies, and its Bristol Tramways & Carriage Company built bodies but also was the group's main supplier of chassis. SMT's Alexander subsidiary built a large proportion of that group's bodywork. State ownership had a fundamental effect on all three manufacturers.

The main British vehicle manufacturers — the likes of Leyland, AEC, Daimler, Guy and Bedford — saw a risk to their businesses. Besides buses, most of the road haulage industry was also being taken into state ownership as British Road Services (BRS). They feared that BTC might meet its requirement for new buses, coaches and lorries from its own factories and they had the legislation amended to prevent BTC factories from supplying any customers other than its own fleets (no other British operators, no exports) and placed a limit on how much of BTC's requirement they could meet.

Tilling was unable to separate ECW and the Bristol manufacturing operations from its sale to BTC, thus stopping them from accepting any new third party orders. Until another Labour government agreed to their partial privatisation in 1965, with Leyland buying a 25% stake, ECW and Bristol (the chassis business was renamed Bristol Commercial Vehicles in 1955) were locked into BTC, building most buses for the fleets in England & Wales, a proportion of those for Scotland, two railbuses for British Railways and Bristol lorries for BRS. ECW also supplied London Transport with 100 bodies and the railway-owned fleets in Sheffield with ten.

SMT only sold its bus operations. The Alexander family formed a new company in 1949 to continue the coachbuilding business which today is the Alexander in leading manufacturer Alexander Dennis. It remained the main supplier of bodywork to the former SMT fleets while also seeking new customers. SMT also retained its car and commercial vehicle dealerships across Scotland.

More major purchases

With area boards very much on its agenda, BTC acquired several operators of significant size. The biggest of these was the 800-vehicle Red & White group with businesses in Gloucestershire, Monmouthshire, south-west Wales, Oxford, Newbury and Basingstoke; it agreed a £4.5million sale in March 1950, worth around £119million in 2021. Other larger businesses to agree takeover terms around the same time were Enterprise of Scunthorpe with 140 vehicles and Youngs of Paisley with 130. It also established a new company, Durham District Services, to mop

BELOW: When SMT sold its bus operations in 1949, the Edinburgh-based SMT company was renamed Scottish Omnibuses but continued to use the original SMT diamond logo as a fleetname until 1964. In July 1962, Alexander-bodied AEC Reliance B906 (YWS 906), new two months earlier, carried both names. It was in Perth, operating the summer express service between Edinburgh and Inverness.
IAIN MacGREGOR

RIGHT: West Riding, one of the last regional bus companies outside a major group, was acquired by the Transport Holding Company in January 1968. It was by far the largest, and almost the only operator of the front-engined Guy Wulfrunian. East Lancs-bodied 959 (XBX 350) had been built for the small West Wales business but was soon bought by West Riding.
IAIN MacGREGOR

BELOW:
MacBraynes, owned jointly by THC and Coast Lines, became 100% owned by the newly created Scottish Transport Group in 1969. Most of its bus operations were absorbed by Scottish Bus Group operators in 1970/71. This was October 3, 1970 when Willowbrook-bodied AEC Reliance 170 (PGE 429F) was departing Glasgow on the company's final working of the service to Campbeltown. Western SMT took over the following day and this bus, like many in the fleet, was transferred to Highland Omnibuses.
IAIN MacGREGOR

up independent operators as it prepared to establish one of the first area boards in north-east England.

BTC placed the Balfour Beatty and Red & White businesses under Tilling control, but in January 1950 transferred the Caledonian Omnibus Company to SBG's Western SMT business which also absorbed the Youngs fleet.

British Railways owned a 50% shareholding in Highland Transport, a 67-vehicle operator serving norther Scotland from Inverness to the north coast, and in September 1951 BTC acquired the other 50%. A month later it added the 28 buses and coaches of Macrae & Dick, based in Inverness and with a presence across other parts of the Highlands. These were merged into a new SBG subsidiary, Highland Omnibuses, in February 1952 along with its existing Alexander's services in and around Inverness.

Although owned by the state, none of this activity was nationalisation in its strictest sense, as the bus companies remained commercial business and were required to trade profitably without state subsidy. That was easier to achieve in 1950 when car ownership was low and buses were often busy, even in country areas. It became a lot more challenging in later decades.

The election of a Conservative government in 1951 brought much of BTC's expansion to an end. Much, but not all, of BRS was

LEFT: British Rail's involvement in Sheffield's municipal bus service allowed it to purchase ECW bodies during the 16 years that the Lowestoft factory could only supply the state-owned sector. The undertaking's railway-owned C and jointly owned B fleets bought ten Leylands with ECW bodies, of which 1294 (YWB 294) in the B fleet was one of five Titan PD2/20s new in 1957. This picture from ten years later shows it passing an Alexander-bodied AEC Regent V in the corporation-owned A fleet.
IAIN MacGREGOR

sold off, often back to the former owners of businesses that had been acquired compulsorily a few years earlier. BTC survived until January 1963, when a new entity, the London-based Transport Holding Company (THC), became the umbrella owner of the Tilling and SBG businesses, BRS, the hotels and Thomas Cook. British Railways and London Transport became boards in their own right.

SBG had been restructured from five to seven subsidiaries in May 1961, when the three areas of the huge Alexander company were reconstituted as free-standing companies.

With Labour back in power from 1964, more radical change followed, with an objective of somehow coordinating public transport. Legislation enacted in 1968 ended BET's fierce resistance to selling its buses to the state, and in November 1967 it bowed to government pressure and agreed the £35million sale of its bus interests in England and Wales (11,000 buses) to the THC, a deal completed in March 1968; that equates to about £450million in 2021. West Riding Automobile sold its 450-bus operation to THC in January 1968 for £1.9million, or £23million today.

However, THC's days were numbered. BRS went to a new National Freight Corporation and from January 1969 the buses and coaches in England and Wales were transferred to the newly created National Bus Company (NBC), while SBG became part of a new Edinburgh-based organisation, the Scottish Transport Group (STG), which also became responsible for shipping services on the Clyde, West Highlands and Western Isles; the Caledonian Steam Packet Company was transferred from what by then was British Rail and STG acquired Coast Lines' shareholding in David MacBrayne (the other half had been in railway ownership for 40 years), which besides ships also ran buses and lorries. Most of MacBraynes' buses were transferred to SBG companies in 1970/71.

THC's 75% shareholding in ECW and Bristol was transferred solely to NBC. This soon developed into a larger joint venture, Bus

BELOW: An early development within the National Bus Company, during 1970, was to divert three ECW-bodied Bristol VRTs ordered by Southern Vectis, the Tilling group company serving the Isle of Wight, to City of Oxford Motor Services, a former BET subsidiary. These were the first Series 2 VRTs built, incorporating improvements made following problems with the first vehicles built in 1968/69, and 903 (OFC 903H) was the third of the trio. They were painted in a simplified version of the traditional Oxford livery on the single-deckers in this September 1970 picture.
IAIN MacGREGOR

ABOVE: South Midland operated the coach service between Oxford and London. A Red & White subsidiary until 1950, it was then managed as a remote offshoot of Thames Valley Traction until 1971 when NBC merged it with City of Oxford. Duple Bella Venture-bodied Bedford VAM14 C414 (GRX 414D) was new in 1966. IAIN MacGREGOR

RIGHT: North Western Road Car 129 (AJA 129B), a Park Royal-bodied AEC Renown new in 1964, was among 272 vehicles sold out of the state-owned sector when the National Bus Company disposed of the subsidiary company's Greater Manchester operations to Selnec PTE in 1972. IAIN MacGREGOR

Manufacturers Holdings (BMH), owned 50/50 by British Leyland and NBC, that also embraced the Park Royal and Charles H Roe bodybuilders that Leyland had acquired with AEC in 1962. BMH also included Leyland National, the jointly owned company established in 1969 to manufacture the standardised rear-engined integral single-decker of the same name at a new factory near Workington; production began towards the end of 1971 with NBC committed

to taking around 500 vehicles a year. Leyland, by then also in state ownership, acquired NBC's shareholding in 1982.

One BET company had built some of its own buses. For decades, Midland Red designed and manufactured vehicles at its central works in Birmingham, but struggled latterly to recruit skilled labour in an area where car manufacturing was booming and driving up pay rates. It produced its last vehicles, single-deckers, in 1970.

NBC adds a subsidiary, merges others

London Transport was moved from state to local control in January 1970, reporting to the Greater London Council, but its country buses and Green Line coaches remained in state ownership, transferred to NBC's new London Country subsidiary. NBC also expanded soon after its formation, acquiring the Provincial company in south Hampshire, Jones of Aberbeeg in south Wales, Venture Transport

in Co. Durham and the small municipal undertakings in Exeter and Luton.

And those railway-owned buses in Yorkshire? NBC created a new subsidiary, Amalgamated Passenger Transport, to take over British Rail's interest in those buses owned directly by the railway. Huddersfield bought NBC's share at the end of 1969, most of Sheffield's NBC-owned buses went to other NBC fleets along with some of the longer routes in January 1970. The arrangements in Halifax and Todmorden lasted until West Yorkshire PTE took over in 1974, by which time most of NBC's Hebble subsidiary's services had come into municipal control.

NBC policy over its first ten years was to merge subsidiaries into larger units. In 1969, Yorkshire Traction absorbed the small Mexborough & Swinton and County Motors businesses, Southern National was merged into Western National (which absorbed Devon General in 1970), Brighton Hove & District was placed under Southdown control (and absorbed completely in 1974) and the western extremity of United Automobile at Carlisle was transferred to Ribble (putting unfamiliar Bristol single-deckers into a predominantly Leyland fleet).

The biggest changes implemented in 1971 were in Wales, where South Wales Transport absorbed United Welsh (another ex-Red & White business) along with Thomas Bros of Port Talbot and the Neath & Cardiff express coach company and Western Welsh absorbed Rhondda Transport (the west Wales operations of Western Welsh transferred to South Wales the following year). Midland Red absorbed its Stratford Blue subsidiary, while the South Midland company (a former Red & White subsidiary operating coaches between Oxford and London) was transferred from Thames Valley to City of Oxford to trade as Oxford South Midland.

Most of this process was completed in 1972. Aldershot & District (ex-BET) and Thames

Valley (ex-Tilling) were merged to become the Thames Valley & Aldershot Omnibus Company, which traded as Alder Valley, a fictitious geographical feature. Hants & Dorset absorbed Wilts & Dorset, East Midland took control of Mansfield District (and absorbed it in 1975), while Trent absorbed Midland General and Notts & Derby.

One last merger followed in 1978 when Western Welsh and Red & White came together as National Welsh which absorbed the small Jones business in 1980.

NBC also agreed to sell parts of two large former BET companies to PTEs. The North Western company's Greater Manchester operations were sold to Selnec PTE in 1972 when 272 buses changed hands, with its remaining bus services in Cheshire and Derbyshire transferred to Crosville and Trent. West Midlands PTE acquired Midland Red's services in the region in December 1973 along with 413 vehicles.

Smaller companies, private buyers

The West Midlands sale was a turning point. There would be no more disposals of urban businesses and NBC cooperated instead with the other four English PTEs, running some buses in PTE-inspired liveries.

The sale also would led to the end of amalgamations and a new belief in the beauty of smaller subsidiaries..

Midland Red tried to make good the loss of its profitable routes in Birmingham and the Black Country by acquiring independent operators in other parts of its territory, including Telford new town, but its financial difficulties mounted and in 1981 NBC took the radical decision to break it up into six separate businesses: four area companies providing bus services in the north, south, east and west of its territory, an express service operator (which lasted just a year) and an engineering company to run its central works.

Such was the success of this move, focusing management on local requirements and opportunities, that NBC's southern region broke up most of its companies into smaller units between 1983 and 1986. In alphabetical order, Alder Valley, Bristol Omnibus Company, City of Oxford, Eastern Counties, Hants & Dorset, Maidstone & District, Southdown, United Counties and Western National were divided into smaller businesses.

It also inspired SBG to take more radical action in 1985, restructuring its bus operations from seven subsidiaries to 11

ABOVE: **By 1984, Leicester-based Midland Red East, one of four local bus companies created out of the National Bus Company's break-up of Midland Red, had been renamed Midland Fox and had a livery on which the only trace of NBC ownership was the double-N logo on the front. MCW-bodied 2917 (KJD 20P) was one of several ex-London Transport DMS-class Leyland Fleetlines that this and other NBC subsidiaries bought on the secondhand market to update their fleets.**
IAIN MacGREGOR

with operating areas determined largely by regional council boundaries; six of the seven companies lost territory, while two of the new companies were each created out of parts of two divided businesses and three other depots were switched between companies.

Neither of these radical changes was a preparation for privatisation, which was not mooted for NBC until 1984 and four years later for SBG. NBC tried to persuade the government to sell it as one business serving all of England & Wales and only conceded defeat early in 1986 after the southern companies had already been divided. However, the government insisted that four companies outside the southern region — London Country, United, Ribble and Crosville — be split up in August and September 1986, just ahead of the deregulation of bus services outside London in October 1986. The opposite happened in Scotland, as SBG turned four of its 11 companies into two larger ones to make them more attractive to buy.

NBC's constituent parts were sold individually between 1986 and 1988 for £324.2million, or about £728million at 2021 prices; in real terms, that was about 60% of the prices paid by BTC and

THC for its major constituent parts. SBG was sold in 1990 and 1991, also in its individual parts, for £103.1million or about £191million at the values of 30 years later; the state paid SMT's shareholders more than three times that in 1949.

The state sector also grew just as privatisation was about to begin. Control of the Greater London Council (GLC) alternated at every election between the Labour and Conservative parties and the relationship between the Conservative government elected in 1979 and the Labour GLC that took power two years later was increasingly fraught, leading to the government taking London Transport back into state ownership in June 1984 under the new name London Regional Transport.

Its London Buses arm was soon exposed to competition as increasing numbers of its routes were opened up to competitive tender, a development that brought early gains for NBC's Eastern National and London Country subsidiaries. Privatisation (and possible deregulation) also was high on the government's agenda, leading to the division of London Buses into separate companies, with the last of these sold in 1994 and early 1995.

The Ulster exception

Thus ended the state ownership of buses in Britain, but not in the fourth country of the United Kingdom, Northern Ireland, where they remain in the public sector today and have been for nearly 90 years. Against its conservative instructs, the province's Unionist government created the Northern Ireland Road Transport Board (NIRTB) in 1935 to try to stem losses on the railways. All bus services other than those operated by Belfast Corporation or on cross-border routes into what then was the Irish Free State were taken over along with much of the road haulage industry.

By the time it completed the acquisitions in June 1936, the NIRTB had nearly 700 buses. It began with the fleets of major operators Belfast Omnibus Company, HMS Catherwood and the LMS (Northern Counties Committee), Belfast & County Down and Great Northern railways; Great Northern continued to operate buses in the free state. Sixty-five other operators' buses were also taken over, some of those operators only providing tours and private hires.

The NIRTB was merged with the railways in September 1948 to form the Ulster Transport Authority (UTA), which was split into separate bus, road freight and railway businesses in April 1967. The bus operation became Ulsterbus, a subsidiary of a newly created Northern Ireland Transport Holding Company (NITHC); the original plan was to divide ownership between the new holding company and the London-based THC, with SBG as its mainland British partner, but the Scottish group — which would be cast free from THC two years later — withdrew from the arrangement shortly before Ulsterbus started operating. A few UTA routes around Portrush and Lurgan were transferred to two private operators in 1967, but Ulsterbus later took over both of those businesses.

The NITHC acquired Belfast Corporation's bus services in April 1973, rebranding them as Citybus. The name has since been changed again to Metro and the body in charge of Ulsterbus, Metro and Northern Ireland Railways is called Translink today. Privatisation has been mooted occasionally but is no longer on the agenda. •

BELOW: **Since January 1994, Translink's Ulsterbus and Metro operations in Northern Ireland have been the UK's only remaining state-owned bus companies. Among recent deliveries to the Ulsterbus fleet for its Goldline interurban services is 1794 (XUI 8090), a low-entry Volvo B8RLE with Sunsundegui Sb3 body built in Spain. This shows it leaving the Europa Buscentre in the heart of Belfast.** PAUL SAVAGE

National white, poppy red and leaf green

Fifty years after the National Bus Company introduced a suite of corporate liveries, MARTIN S CURTIS recalls their introduction and considers if the reaction they provoked was justified

RIGHT: The cover of the National Bus Company's 1972 annual report, showing scenes from a television advertisement filmed in Aldershot, including the double-N formation.

Fifty years ago in 1972, Freddie Wood, the recently appointed chairman of the National Bus Company, announced plans for a new corporate approach to be applied to the structure and appearance of the organisation. The look of bus services across England and Wales was changed forever.

At its formation in January 1969, NBC brought together 21,760 buses and coaches of the former Tilling and BET groups of regional bus companies, many of which also operated express coach services together with excursions and tours. Several express networks — such as those of Royal Blue — were extensive, while others were subject to careful coordination through bodies such as Associated Motorways.

Many expected the traditional identities and names of constituent companies to remain, as they had under private ownership and, in the case of Tilling, during the previous 20 years of state control. Most of the Tilling fleets had a standard livery of either the same shade of red or green, complemented by one or more band of cream. Most BET fleets also had liveries of either red or green, but the shades varied, as did the application of a relief colour.

At its inception, NBC was composed of 62 operating companies and during the summer of 1972 I began my career with one of them, Bristol Omnibus Company, where locally there was yet to be any hint of corporate liveries. Coaches were a different matter as, in early 1970, NBC's south-west region headed by director JTE Robinson, had introduced revised coach liveries of white with a different colour waistband, on which was a prominent fleetname in Eurostile Bold Extended typeface.

This scheme cleverly reinforced the company names while displaying a strong family connection between the fleets, with relief colours of black for

Black & White, magenta for Bristol Greyhound, turquoise for Greenslades, pale grey for Grey Cars and dark blue for Royal Blue.

A group-wide coach livery

The first indication of a corporate livery for coaches nationwide was revealed in April 1972 when Freddie Wood showed the press a coach painted white and carrying large block capital letter National names in a style similar to Haas Helvetica Bold with each character in alternate red or blue. A new red and blue double-N symbol was also displayed.

It was implied that the new brand would appear in combination with individual company names, and since these had built up such a strong public following, it was not immediately clear at this point how this arrangement would work. It seemed unthinkable that names such as Black & White Motorways, Crosville, Eastern Counties, Midland Red, Standerwick and Yorkshire Traction, with their well-known express networks, would not remain prominent, while Ribble, Southdown, Western Welsh and others had long established high-quality tours programmes.

However, Wood had become familiar with the Greyhound brand across America and wanted to mirror this with a single

name for coach travel across the country. Britain had a myriad of inter-connecting express coach services, but to access them passengers had to either know the operator's name, or approach their local company to unravel the complexities of connections which might involve a transfer at bus or coach stations, the largest of which were at Cheltenham and London Victoria.

Other changes were occurring too. Britain's motorway network was growing rapidly, allowing faster journey times but with fewer intermediate stops, while British Rail was also improving

competing services on some routes, with its new InterCity 125 High Speed Trains introduced from 1976.

Accordingly, it gradually became clear that every NBC subsidiary was required to repaint its coaches into white, with initially a tiny — almost indistinguishable — company name in grey (underlined in the company's colour) placed over the front wheels. This move was far from universally popular and resistance to the changes in some companies was considerable.

A small concession was made later in 1972 when the company

ABOVE: One of NBC's first steps towards a corporate livery was on coaches in the west of England, painted western white with a coloured waistband and fleetnames in a new typeface. Bristol Greyhound adopted a distinctive magenta, as on ECW-bodied RELH6G 2130 (976 WAE) which had stopped at Marlborough for a refreshment break. MSC COLLECTION

LEFT: The original small company fleetname over the front wheel of Maidstone & District 2541 (BKT 804C), a 49-seat dual purpose Weymann bodied AEC Reliance, at Victoria Coach Station in London in September 1972. The thick underline was green. ALAN MILLAR

ABOVE: Crosville CRG531 (AFM 106B), an ECW-bodied Bristol RELH6G, with the larger company fleetname applied in this case to the illuminated house glass over the front wheel. In September 1978, it had strayed from the National network, borrowed by Western SMT to operate one of its all-stops services between Glasgow and Ayr.
IAIN MacGREGOR

name over the front wheels was increased in size but this now appeared everywhere in red with no underlining. Absurdly, names such as Black & White and Royal Blue were displayed in anything

but the correct colours. To make matters worse, and following no logic, some fleetnames were shortened with the result that Maidstone & District became Maidstone and Bristol Greyhound

lost Greyhound, leaving only the city name. These titles on coach sides looked like destinations but were not necessarily where the coaches were heading.

In locations such as Cheltenham and Victoria, confusion among travellers was compounded by more vehicles appearing in white rather than liveries that regular customers were used to. While on one hand National white emphasised the huge network of routes, on the ground it was not entirely welcomed by passengers and staff because of the lack of attention to these details as the transition occurred.

A further puzzling consequence of the decision to remove the Greyhound name was its timing. Greyhound Motors' inauguration of its Bristol-London service in 1925 was regarded as the world's first express coach service of its kind and this was something about to be celebrated during the 50th anniversary year in 1975.

Drip-feeding the changes
For most NBC employees, the news of the extension of a corporate image to local buses came with the second edition of *bus*, a new eight-page staff newspaper. To be produced five times a year, this was meant to draw the group together with stories from around the country.

Arguably, it fell at the first hurdle because only one page

RIGHT: The front page of the second NBC staff newspaper dated July 1972, announcing changes to local bus liveries across the country.

in each edition was devoted to the local operator's news and, simultaneously, companies were instructed to cease publication of their own house magazines. Some of the latter were of a very high standard and had been produced and collected for decades, so while the new paper represented an economy, staff saw it as a poor substitute.

Issue No2, dated July 1972, carried the headline "Buses to get new look" and explained that local company fleetnames would now be carried in 5in high NBC-style lettering together with the NBC symbol. This would appear in cream on existing liveries but gradually would change to white with each fleet's main colour. The story was accompanied by images of Alder Valley buses, a company recently created by the merger of ex-Tilling Thames Valley and former BET Aldershot & District. In this case a new cherry red livery had been adopted as this was one of six standard colours proposed for NBC fleets.

The assumption was that the established shades of green, red or blue of many operators would be adapted to include the new-style names. This was not the case and as if the full details were being revealed incrementally to soften the blow, the next revelation came at the Earls Court Commercial Motor Show in London in September. On display

were three NBC service buses, two double-deck and one single-deck.

The double-deckers were a Leyland Atlantean for London Country and a Bristol VRT for Southern Vectis, but instead of wearing those operators' respective shades of Lincoln or Tilling green, they were in a pale shade which looked even lighter under the Earls Court spotlights. The single-decker was a Bristol LH for Eastern Counties in a very strange light red, with no white relief whatsoever. They looked awful and not only failed to impress visitors to the show, but also received extensive criticism in the trade press.

However, these revised hues were apparently to be the new

NBC standards. Among others, they would sweep away Tilling green and red, Midland General blue, the deep reds of Ribble and Western Welsh and possibly the most popular of them all, Southdown apple green.

A bold move

Obliterating long established liveries was a bold move by NBC, which took the unusual step of running a television advertising campaign to promote its new corporate image. Filmed in Aldershot during late September, it was broadcast the next month and into November.

In addition to a single white coach, 33 service buses from around the country (the farthest traveling from Tyneside) were

RIGHT: The poppy red NBC local coach livery on West Yorkshire Road Car 1011 (MWR 963D), an ECW-bodied Bristol RELH6G.
IAIN MacGREGOR

BELOW: Before NBC applied its corporate identity, Midland General double-deckers were blue and cream while single-deckers were cream and black. It was one of the handful of fleets to have the blue version of the standard livery, which it soon replaced with poppy red as the company's operations were merged into Trent's. This April 1973 picture shows recently repainted Bristol Lodekka FLF6G 751 (YNU 350G), the second last Lodekkas built in 1968, outside the garage of former sister company Mansfield District which adopted the leaf green version of the new livery in place of green with cream window surrounds, as is evident on the two Lodekka FS6Gs on the right. East Midland, which absorbed the Mansfield District business, adopted leaf green and white in place of its previous dark red.
MSC COLLECTION

ABOVE: Hants & Dorset 1834 (2688 RU), an ECW-bodied Bristol MW6G coach downgraded to a service bus, at Bournemouth Bus Station during the summer of 1975 in the intermediate livery of Tilling green and cream, with cream fleetnames and double-N symbol.
MARTIN S CURTIS

assembled to create a series of fast moving sequences with green and red buses passing and crossing with a clever aerial shot from a helicopter, depicting buses in formation to create a double-N. This was seen so briefly in the finished production that it was difficult to appreciate, but stills from the day later appeared on the cover of the 1972 NBC annual report.

The new shades were officially known as poppy red and leaf green with a final modification to the liveries being the inclusion of light grey wheels – possibly not the most practical colour for service buses. However, few vehicles had yet to receive the new NBC liveries.

Many of the Aldershot participants were hurriedly modified with new fleetnames and white bands applied on old colours and at least 12 came from the nearby Alder Valley fleet. These comprised a Marshall-bodied Bristol RE and five Dennis Lolines, all still wearing Aldershot & District green, while a VRT and four more Lolines were in Alder Valley dark red. The lead bus was an Alder Valley ECW-bodied RE, also in dark red. Among the remaining participants were Bristol Omnibus, Crosville, East Midland, London Country, Midland Red, Northern General, Red & White, Ribble, South Wales, Yorkshire Traction, West Yorkshire and Western National.

By the end of 1972, most subsidiaries had begun repainting vehicles in the new red or green shades, with non-front line coaches, previously termed dual-purpose, receiving a local coach scheme of fleet colour below the waist and white above. The new colours received a mixed reaction from an industry steeped in its history and traditions.

One NBC senior manager suggested that before long the new colours would be as well liked as the old. He was wrong; and one cause for this was the quality of the new paints. Paint shop staff were heard to say, "The new paint has no depth to it", while the lighter hues did not suit older bus designs. It could look smart when freshly applied, but seemed to fade rapidly which affected several red fleets terribly. At least one company changed

supplier which reduced this issue and there was certainly a difference in appearance between fleets.

For those vehicles not immediately due for a repaint, attempts were made to paint out cream relief and apply new fleetnames over old, which in many cases resulted in a dishevelled appearance. This did nothing to enhance NBC's image.

It should also be remembered that 50 years ago a far higher proportion of the population (certainly outside London) used local bus services than today. Buses were a big part of many people's daily lives and it mattered how they looked. For most towns and cities they were an intrinsic component of the local scene, reflecting its identity and did much to publicly characterise locations; staff also were part of something tangible, relating to their particular area. Locations with lots of buses had regularly been associated with their liveries, but this would now be largely lost forever.

A few operators persisted with the use of blue – applied in NBC style. These included East Yorkshire, Sunderland District and Midland General. The small south Wales fleet of Jones of Aberbeeg was a fourth, but while the others gradually succumbed to poppy red, somehow Jones managed to retain blue until

ABOVE: NBC
liveries reached
rock bottom when
a few subsidiaries
dispensed with white
relief as an economy.
Crosville was one
such company, with
not only a lack of
waistband, but also
green grille, wings
and advertisement
panel as exemplified
by Bristol Lodekka
FS6G DFG38
(319 PFM). The
poor condition of
paintwork reflects
a low standard of
appearance overall
which was unlikely
to encourage
passengers to switch
to public transport.
MSC COLLECTION

1980. Another exception was on Tyneside, where in order to display coordination with PTE buses, both United and Northern vehicles operating in that area were painted yellow, in NBC style.

NBC's corporate identities then spread to include every aspect of operations, with double-N symbols appearing on new uniforms, publicity, buildings, stationery and more. By 1977 the double-N on service buses had switched from white to red and blue in a white box, which was a surprisingly effective improvement.

However, some operators removed white bands from their livery as an economy, with appalling results. In Wales, bilingual fleetnames appeared with English or Welsh versions displayed on opposite sides.

After the dust had settled
In due course, some fleets were merged together and others absorbed into larger concerns. Many of NBC's coaching activities were removed from

subsidiaries and formed into regional coaching units. Express coach services saw the name National Express gradually appear on publicity and then as a fleetname instead of plain National.

From October 1980, deregulation of express services brought competition to the market and rival express coach firms ventured into express operations; new concerns continue to provide alternative services today, with varying success. The emphasis on a National Express network remained, however, and 50 years after its introduction, the name is still with us, indicating that for this sector, the corporate image was successful.

A National Holidays brand was also developed and when NBC

was broken up and disposed of between 1986 and 1988, National Holidays was the first unit to be sold; its new owner dropped the brand after a few years, but it was revived by a new-start business and the name has since changed hands several times.

The local bus industry has adjusted differently. Many questioned how important the benefits might be if local buses in Cumbria looked like those in south Wales or Kent. There was a constant urge to break away from corporate doctrines and given any opportunity – usually associated with marketing campaigns or projects — many new local names and identities were introduced for small groups of services. Nevertheless, few of these made a lasting impact.

They couldn't wait

New owners of former NBC companies could not wait to establish new liveries, many reviving those lost in 1972. Curiously, this was often welcomed by staff, local communities and all levels of government, which provides an interesting contrast to the previous decade and may have been linked to a new optimism which was lacking with the NBC approach.

The bus industry is ever changing, however, and by the 1990s new groups of operators began to appear with companies joining together once more. The two largest groups at this point were Stagecoach, which again applied a corporate identity to replace the newly revived local schemes, and

BELOW: Newport bus station was the setting for this June 1977 scene with Jones, Aberbeeg R3671 (YWO 691K), an ECW-bodied Bristol RELL6L new six years earlier. Against all expectations, this small south Wales fleet clung on to blue livery until National Welsh absorbed it in 1980. This has the later version of the double-N logo, in red and blue on a white background.
MARTIN S CURTIS

Badgerline which initially allowed strong local identities but with discreet group insignia, and from my own experience the latter approach appeared successful with not only staff and customers, but also local authorities which could relate to its local operator. However, the 1995 merger of Badgerline with GRT Bus Group to create First took this group in an altogether different direction

Half a century on from NBC's corporate approach, bus services relate less clearly to areas or regions. Patronage has fallen generally although there are some notable exceptions, while for many reasons ridership increased in London, which was separate from NBC's activities.

Initially, NBC's privatisation fragmented operations once more – and while some were gradually drawn into new groups, none is as dominant as NBC. Today, the Stagecoach and Arriva approach of unified countrywide liveries is not conducive to a local following.

Go-Ahead and First have taken the opposite path and it could be argued that that maintains greater loyalty among passengers and staff, who feel a connection with an identifiable operator.

The industry currently has many challenges. Work to restore patronage may benefit from a glance back 50 years to remind us of the corporate measures then taken by NBC, how their acceptance varied greatly and whether they led to ultimate success. •

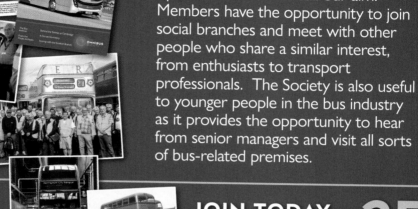

What **NBC** taught me

ABOVE: Typical of the rolling stock still on the daily roster when James Freeman first went to Swansea was 879 (GWN 857D), a Willowbrook-bodied AEC Regent V photographed in Princess Way in September 1977.
ALAN MILLAR

JAMES FREEMAN joined the National Bus Company's management training scheme when he graduated from university in 1978, developing skills that helped him make a successful career in the industry over the next 40-plus years

The National Bus Company (NBC) inherited the management training schemes of its two main constituents. Both BET and the Transport Holding Company ran well-developed programmes to develop future managers.

They were brought together by the new NBC team and by the time I first had contact with the organisation in 1972, it had a well-established and clear programme under which about a dozen young people — usually but not necessarily graduates — were recruited each September for a two-year training scheme.

Each was allocated to one of the operating companies, with the whole group brought together for specialist courses. Their progress was monitored carefully by a Senior Management Training Scheme (SMTS) committee, chaired by an NBC director, which required each trainee to write a detailed monthly report on what they had seen and learned, and summoned them to London every six months to be grilled by the committee. That was a scary process, and no mistake.

Assuming good progress was made, the trainee could expect a first appointment to be in a quite different company (usually in another part of the country) in a junior management post. After that, individuals' progress was their own to determine, but many became leaders in the industry.

NBC's leadership set considerable store by its training scheme which was part of a coherent programme to build a team of future leaders. The success of this aim was amply demonstrated by the dominant role of so many NBC trainees in the privatisation process in 1986-88. Several were able to retire on the proceeds of the subsequent sales – not quite the outcome that was intended when they were recruited on to the scheme but certainly a sign that the scheme had developed the necessary skills and abilities.

Careers advice

My own involvement started as I moved into the sixth form and sat in front of the teacher who was in charge of careers advice. He was a little perplexed by my telling him I wanted to make my career in the bus industry — "in the *what* industry?" — but consummate professional that he was, he made enquiries and not long afterwards I was in the lobby of NBC's headquarters, 25 New Street Square, off New Fetter Lane in London EC4, waiting to see the training development officer, Malcolm Blanksby.

Our discussion was wide-ranging and enjoyable, but his advice at the end was to do well at my A-levels and then get a degree in a subject that I wanted. Meanwhile, I should take a year off to find out about the business at the sharp end. I was to stay in touch. I still am in touch with him, 50 years later.

Malcolm was as good as his word. With A-levels behind me in the summer of 1974, he recommended a year out, with six months "on the back" as a conductor and the rest of the year in the office somewhere. He made the introductions and I was taken on by Hants & Dorset as a conductor at Winchester, starting on September 1, 1974. I stayed there until March 1975 and in those six months accumulated a huge stack of experiences that stood me in good stead throughout my career.

Then I switched to the traffic administration department of the Bristol Omnibus Company, based at its Bristol headquarters, Berkeley House, on the edge of the massive Lawrence Hill complex. Here I encountered a whole range of different experiences and formed some long-standing friendships.

After three years at Southampton University, where I read history (and including going back to Bristol Omnibus for a summer vacation in 1977) it was time for the "milk round" when big employers would interview potential candidates for the various training schemes.

MANAGEMENT CAREERS IN THE BUS AND COACH INDUSTRY

NATIONAL BUS COMPANY

THE PEOPLE MOVERS

At Southampton, this was delegated to the two local general managers, PC Hunt of Hants & Dorset and Michael Wadsworth of Southern Vectis.

I remember that it was a daunting but in the event most energising and exciting interview and it must have worked because I was offered a place on the SMTS to start in September 1978. They warned me that I would most likely be allocated to a company in a different part of the country from my home and experience, but I had to wait to find out where.

Posted to South Wales Transport

I clearly remember the arrival of the envelope, postmarked "Swansea, West Glamorgan" that told me I was to report to the South Wales Transport (SWT) traffic manager, Stuart Senior, at 09:00 on my first day, at the start of September 1978. The train journey from Slough (near where I lived at then) to Swansea was an experience, as I sat and anticipated what I would be doing. But it all started as it would go on: I was met at the station by David Park, the depot superintendent for the main

ABOVE: Cover of the brochure with which NBC tried to attract graduating students on to its management training scheme.

depots in Swansea, Brunswick Street and Ravenhill.

He drove me to the Mumbles in his company Mini, where I was to be put up in a (very pleasant) guest house until I found myself a flat. It was a beautiful Sunday afternoon at the end of the holidays and I was struck by the number of full double-deckers we passed, bringing people back from a day on the beach at what I soon came to know as "the Bays".

The next two years were filled with a programme carefully devised by NBC to give each trainee an all-round grounding in the business. It involved attachments to all three disciplines in the business — operations, engineering and secretarial — including lots of opportunities for the trainees to get their hands dirty as well as (later on in the course) "training in responsibility", which was standing in for managers who were on holiday or sick. It also was a wonderful opportunity to get to know a new part of the country, itself a most rewarding experience.

Before I got stuck into the programme, I spent a day with each area manager. During my day with the area manager West, Robin Orbell, he attended a bus stop site meeting in a village on the way to Carmarthen. I was just an observer, but it was a spectacular example of how tricky simple things can be. A bus stop needed to be moved, but it was as if the whole cast of Dylan Thomas's *Under Milk Wood* had turned up, as different traders and local authority officers to say nothing of the public – and

LEFT: The training vehicle on which James Freeman stepped on the brake on Fairwood Common, Willowbrook-bodied AEC Regent V 54 (999 BCY), which had been new in 1962.
GEOFF GOULD

of course the bus company – slugged it out on site in the street.

I was fascinated to watch how Robin sought to guide the ructions round so that we got the bus stop to a location that worked for our passengers and drivers. He managed it and I have often thought back to that day when dealing with angry stakeholders in one situation or another: always let them have their say and listen properly. Always explain carefully and honestly and then seek to get a consensus before agreeing on the outcome. Anyway, I digress...

A grounding in schedules

The NBC programme laid down that the first 12 weeks were spent in the schedules office. The purpose of this lengthy immersion in what was quite a technical area of the business was that to be an effective bus manager you needed to learn how to create good schedules. At the same time, the trainee got to know the network and the layout of the company and its principal people at every location. This scheduling insight has always proved a handy asset to me.

Twelve weeks, though, felt like an impossibly long time to a keen raw recruit, but it provided a calm base from which to get acclimatised. The schedulers were kind to me. There were four of them, each with their own idiosyncrasies, but all very skilled and capable. I was soon to learn that schedulers are special people, each with their own approach and often sceptical (sometimes very much so) of the skills of other schedulers. These days they are in short supply and whatever computers can do, there is nothing like the good eye of a skilled scheduler to spot how to make nice schedules and rosters that are good to work and efficient in cost terms.

I was impressed that the schedules clerk who was responsible for the big Swansea depots had arthritis of the fingers, bearing in mind that all the duty cards were handwritten. He had evolved a shorthand that had to be learnt by all the crews if they were to make head or tail of their instructions. They did, and it worked, somehow.

I moved next into licensing, then a very important section, as maintaining all the road service licences and dealing with the traffic commissioner, including preparing for traffic court hearings, was vital to the company's survival.

This was a different kettle of fish. Whereas the schedules office was on the sunny side of the building (which meant that a lot of the afternoon was spent dozing on sunny days as the room quickly resembled a tomato house), the licensing office was on the east side. I was intrigued to find that the licensing officer was good at his job but absolutely disengaged from the business. I already knew more about where the buses went than he did, despite his 30 years' service.

Most of the social interaction in that office was in Welsh, which to a young English trainee took a bit of getting used to. Yet I forged a relationship with these people over

those weeks and was still in touch with some of them years later.

I duly went round the other head office operating functions, such as marketing and publicity, before joining a depot and seeing what life was like within a particular location. For me, this was the first opportunity to get to know the people who drove and conducted the buses, as well as the supervisors and managers. My first morning in Brunswick Street's output office,

where all the crews signed on, was a revelation as I watched the controller juggling people and buses to get everything covered and then account for what had been done.

Each morning was an exhausting session, but the controllers were experienced and nothing seemed to faze them, even though they tended to be especially heavy smokers as one way of dealing with the stress. I was so impressed to see how they

knew their people and how to coax the best out of them.

It was here that I learned that the company secretary, Leslie Beynon, a clever man who I think had made a lifestyle decision to stay in Swansea — otherwise I am sure he would have been a leading light in NBC's financial team in London — had introduced an excellent control system for allocating drivers' time. I have never seen anything to rival it. Every paid minute was neatly and thoroughly accounted for every day. This made sure that everybody got paid correctly for what they did and all wasted time could be (and was) identified for future action.

Learn to drive

Next was the driving school. This was an exciting moment. The licence I gained then is still current as I write this and I still make use of it regularly.

My first experience was a defining one. As a group of new trainees, we were taken out on to nearby Fairwood Common on board one of the training buses, 999 BCY, a Willowbrook-bodied AEC Regent V typical of the 1960s SWT fleet. I was sent into the driving seat for my first tentative stint behind the wheel. The instructor leant through from the saloon and said: "When I say stop, do so.".

What he did not know was that the only bus I had ever driven up to that point was a 1933 Renault TN6A from Paris, owned by my friend Robert E Jowitt. On that vehicle, to make it stop, you had to push with all your might on the brake pedal. So when he said "Stop!" I did just that on the AEC. Fitted with effective air brakes, it stopped more or less dead. All the other trainees found themselves variously splattered against the front bulkheads. The instructor put his head through the window and commented laconically: "You won't do that again, boyo!" I did not.

I passed my test after lessons with a wonderful trainer. Ronnie Frohwein had been a bus driver for many years but had turned into a marvellous and patient tutor, who had an enviably high pass rate for his students, including me. He taught on a Bristol Lodekka LD ex-Midland General. I am so glad I learned on a crash-box Bristol. To be taught how to manipulate the gears from first principles was a great benefit and I am still today called upon to drive old Bristols of which younger drivers are often scared, whereas I love them.

Armed with a licence, I was keen to get some live experience on the road. The trade union at SWT was the Transport & General Workers. It had a reputation for being quite militant and managers had never been allowed to drive, but it agreed that I could take the place of a paid employee as long as they could just go home on full pay. This suited everybody and I was soon able to do quite a bit of driving in the evenings and at weekends, at first as a crew driver (I enjoyed driving the Regents) and then later one-manning (as it

was then called). They got so used to seeing me behind the wheel that I was able to so some jobs in my own right.

As a manager, I have always valued my ability to drive a bus. To be clear, I am not a "cab happy" manager, the ones who prefer to drive a bus than solve a problem, but I have found, repeatedly, that colleagues like to see the boss of a bus company out there and experiencing life at the sharp end for real, once in a while. I have managed to do it everywhere I have been and it always has an electric effect on how the driving staff view us. In meetings with staff and with politicians and officials and with the public, it always pays to be able to say, "I know from my own experience that such-and-such is true...". It never failed to impress. Apart from anything else, there is an implied compliment to the drivers there: what is good enough for you is good enough for me. Deeds often speak louder than words.

How I became Quadrant Man
Then came the opening of the Quadrant bus station in Swansea in 1979. The council had built a big new bus station to replace an old coach station and buses terminating on city centre streets. The change involved the closure of one of Swansea's three depots, Clarence Terrace, and the wholesale reallocation of work across the city. It was a once-in-a-lifetime change in routes and times and schedules and work patterns, and it all happened on the same day.

The Sunday went off well enough but by about 14:00 on the Monday it was fast becoming apparent that something was seriously wrong. The parking area of the bus station was thronged with parked buses and the canteen was standing room only, but departures were missing and arriving crews were not being relieved. I happened still to be in the operating department at the time and I cannot remember

BELOW: **James Freeman and inspector Tom Davies of SWT sitting at the desk in Gorseinon outstation, otherwise known as Park Royal-bodied AEC Regent V 598 (431 HCY).** TW BAKER

how it happened, but by the Monday afternoon, armed with a clipboard, I was setting to work to run the service by marrying up the crews and available buses – running up and down what became (to me) an ever bigger bus station. If ever there was a seat-of-the-pants operation, this was it.

And when we had got through Monday, there was Tuesday. From Tuesday and right through the week, with the help of the controllers on duty, I ran the whole operation from my clipboard, making it up as we went along. I relied on the drivers and conductors to do what I asked, and to my surprise, they did and willingly. We broke all kinds of agreed processes but all to get the buses running. Nobody seemed to mind. They just got on with it.

In the meantime, the senior management was re-writing the schedules in the background for introduction the following Monday. In a week, I wore out a pair of shoes but we had kept the buses on the road and I had

established a reputation across the company that stayed with me all the time I remained at SWT. It was a key moment in my career: I realised that you could get colleagues to do almost anything as long as you explain what you need and they know you are in it with them.

After that week, anything else was going to be a bit of an anticlimax, but I was off to Ravenhill works for an attachment to the engineering department. My reputation had gone before me: "Oh, you're the Quadrant man! We've heard all about that". As a result, I could get really into understanding how life worked for the engineers and trying to get an insight into the age-old antipathy between engineers and drivers, with many engineers subscribing to the theory: "We fix them and you break 'em".

Often the problems lie in the absence of communication and understanding and the fact that engineering managers are often technically competent but not

people people. In my experience, too little attention is focused on dealing with the engineers as people.

Secretarial and responsibility

There followed three months in secretarial. This was necessary but the time passed slowly and, to be honest, the numbers in the four-weekly returns never really spoke to me until they were my numbers. Then it was different.

Suffice it to say that SWT's accounts department was extremely well run and efficient. They also showed me, with considerable pride, their mainframe computer in the basement of 31 Russell Street. It helped them pay the wages. All that processing is now done in something the size of the wristwatch. What a difference in a lifetime.

The programme included a period of training in responsibility. This was the opportunity for young trainee managers to try their hands at being in charge. Here I was lucky.

BELOW: The Shamrock & Rambler coach fleet included two Bova Futuras new in June 1984. By 1985, in a livery for The Bournemouth Orchestras, 3124 had been re-registered 124 YTW.
IAIN MacGREGOR

Rather than just sitting in for managers who went on holiday, I was sent to a small depot outside Swansea called Gorseinon. Hitherto managed by Peter Heath, who was based several miles farther west in Llanelli, it was felt that there needed to be a local management presence to oversee a planned downgrading to an outstation. This involved redeploying admin staff and/or making them redundant.

It also meant selecting the supervisor who was to lead the depot in its new format, based in an AEC Regent double-decker converted into a (very cosy) depot office. We had three inspectors but one of them was an older man who seemed to have lost his mojo. Yet, as I got to know the three of them, I saw a spark in him which I thought was worth pursuing. In due course, he became the inspector-in-charge at Gorseinon. Overnight, he came alive. He took on the role of guiding the drivers through the traumatic changeover and setting up the new arrangements. He worked hard and with gusto – he had a wonderful time.

For me, it was a super lesson in how to identify people with potential who are under-used and underperforming. If you can light a fire in their belly then all you have to do is guide them and they will do the rest. That was what happened in Gorseinon back in 1979/80.

Running my own company

At the end of my two years, I was expecting to be sent away to the opposite end of the country but my then general manager had other ideas. He told NBC I was to stay in SWT. So I did, for another two years, learning all the time.

It was not too long until I was managing my own NBC company. Hants & Dorset had been split up and one of the spin-offs was Shamrock & Rambler Coaches of Bournemouth. They could not find a manager, so I went there in 1983 when I was just 27, in charge of 120 people and 40 coaches. It was the great chance to put into practice what I had learned, which was that what

James Freeman – Manager, Shamrock and Rambler Coaches

One of my main reasons for joining NBC was that I wanted a career which would involve me with people of all kinds. And one of the first things I learned was that the bus industry contains many highly-committed and well-motivated people. Another major attraction for me was the varied quality of life in the constantly changing transport world – in which each successive day is at least slightly different from the last. Somehow I didn't fancy a routine life.

As a trainee I was sent first of all to South Wales Transport, one of the smaller companies, based in Swansea. It was an experience in itself to move to South Wales and to get to know the district. I made many friends in the Swansea area – friends with whom I've kept in touch ever since.

When I started, the two year Training Scheme seemed to stretch endlessly into the future. But the time went by all-too-quickly. First I got to know the Company in general, and then I spent time on every section of the business, traffic planning, operating, maintenance, central workshops, administration, accounts. By the end of my training I knew the way each department worked, and how it fitted into the whole. I came to understand how the Company could not operate without all its constituent elements working together.

After the first year I really began to settle in, and suddenly I began to find that others had confidence in me and treated me as part of the team. And I had tried my hand at about every duty from driving to sitting-in on important management meetings. There were opportunities to take responsibility, too. I ran a small depot for several months when the Superintendent went sick – valuable experience which I was able to put to good use later on.

Unusually, my first appointment after completing the Training Scheme was to the Traffic Department of South Wales Transport itself. After a few months of general duties I took part in the creation of a new Coaching Unit and was subsequently appointed Coaching Officer. I had the stimulating task of assimilating part of another local undertaking, just acquired, into a coherent coaching operation when coaching had recently been 'deregulated'. This was life at the "sharp end", as we grappled with many new problems. My personnel skills were necessarily sharpened to bring the staff together into a cohesive, committed team – the first operating season was quite a test and very hard work, but very rewarding, too.

My next move was to National Holidays, as 'Field Operations Manager' for South East England. This was a very different sort of job, with responsibility for ensuring that all National Holidays operations in South East worked properly. It involved a great deal of negotiation with NBC operating companies, and with individual drivers and other members of staff. I found it very exciting to work in a Company which was quickly earning its place as market leader in coach holidays, and sobering to think that the enjoyment of thousands of people depended on the arrangements that I had made.

Several new NBC companies have emerged in recent years, and about eighteen months ago I was appointed Manager of Shamrock & Rambler Coaches in Bournemouth. My training in Swansea really comes into its own now. Shamrock & Rambler is a small Company, but running it involves all the challenges of managing a full-sized undertaking. I am responsible to the board of Directors for achieving successful results. I have to lead a management team covering all the disciplines – traffic, engineering and administrative. Together we plan budgets, set our targets and work towards them. The days are often long, but I have the satisfaction of being my own master and leader of a varied team of people.

The seven years since I joined the Training Scheme have passed quickly. I little thought when I joined the NBC Training Scheme that I would be managing a Company before I was 28!

mattered most was looking after the people – being honest with them, good and bad, leading from the front and demonstrating passion and enthusiasm.

At the same time, we needed to take commercial decisions that improved performance. I remember the thrill of the first year that we got the firm back into profit. The most important thing was that we all needed to believe in ourselves.

The SMTS gave me a thorough grounding in the basics of bus operation. But not just me: each year a dozen people were taken on and the majority of them made it through, and NBC was starting to get the benefit of a whole raft of ambitious, clever,

knowledgeable managers to run its businesses.

It was not its fault that privatisation came along in 1986 and broke it all up. So I always maintain a soft spot for National Bus. It trained me as a manager and it trained me well. That stood me in good stead as my career progressed, most recently as chief executive officer of Reading Buses and latterly as managing director of First West of England. I have greatly enjoyed this time.

It is odd, therefore, that the fashion in the big group companies these days is to select managers with no knowledge of how to run buses. I wonder whether that is really such a good thing. But that is another story. •

ABOVE: The 1984 brochure promoting the NBC management training scheme included a page in which James Freeman charted his seven-year route from raw recruit to running Shamrock & Rambler.

Bristol Omnibus

Despite its name, the Bristol Omnibus Company — in state ownership from 1948 — served a much wider part of the west of England than just the city itself. MARTIN S CURTIS recalls its activities in the 1970s when he began his bus industry career there.

Bristol Tramways & Carriage Company, a Tilling group subsidiary, had a huge operating territory covering a far greater area than Bristol itself.

This stretched north to Hereford, Great Malvern and Evesham, east to Oxford and Hungerford and south to Salisbury and Bridgwater. To the west, Bristol Tramways services reached the banks of the Bristol Channel and River Severn, running from Highbridge to Sharpness, and crossed over to the Forest of Dean connecting with Chepstow and Monmouth.

It operated over 1,360 vehicles when it became state-owned in 1948, and the Tilling company structure of regional companies remained after that, although a few boundary adjustments

were made and the Red & White group's Cheltenham District Traction Company came under Bristol control. Cheltenham's dark red buses made a striking contrast to those of Bristol Tramways and its existing subsidiaries, Bath Electric Tramways and Bath Tramways Motor Company, which had all adopted Tilling green and cream from the end of World War Two.

Since it no longer operated trams, Bristol Tramways was renamed Bristol Omnibus Company in 1957, but it was still run much as it always had been when the National Bus Company (NBC) came into existence in January 1969. A year later, in January 1970, Bristol Omnibus took over the operations of Western National, another former Tilling concern, in the Trowbridge and Chippenham areas of Wiltshire, which were

distant from Western National's Exeter head office.

One consequence of this was that for many years thereafter, staff there remained members of the National Union of Railwaymen (NUR) — now the Rail Maritime & Transport (RMT) union —while most Bristol Omnibus employees were Transport & General Workers Union (TGWU) members.

It was into this environment that I joined Bristol Omnibus in 1972 and spent ten years there, gaining a thorough grounding in the activities of a bus operator.

Bristol was among Britain's oldest public transport providers, and generated considerable pride among many of its staff at all levels. It was steeped in history, with tales handed down from generation to generation. A young teenager joining as a tramways points boy in the 1920s would still be recounting stories

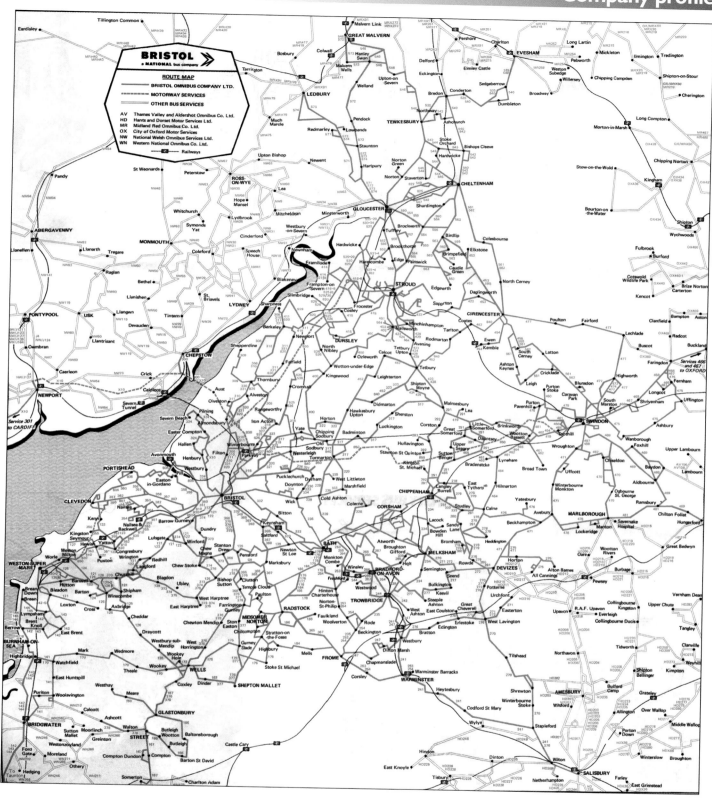

ABOVE: The Bristol Omnibus network map during the NBC era.

of that time to his colleagues half a century later as OMO (one-man operation, the term then used) with the latest rear-engined buses was being introduced on urban services.

The company and its staff formed a hugely important part of city life in Bristol, and in the other towns, cities and countryside in its operating area. But it was not without its problems.

Severe staff shortages prevailed and difficulties in obtaining sufficient spare parts for vehicles were surfacing. Services in some locations were becoming unreliable as a result; private car ownership was increasing while passenger numbers declined, and the fleet had already shrunk to just over 1,200 buses. Nevertheless, there was a lot going on at Bristol Omnibus.

A new headquarters

In 1970, a new office block, Berkeley House, opened adjacent to Lawrence Hill depot and central repair works to become Bristol Omnibus Company's new headquarters. Previously, head office had been in the heart of the city, at 1-3 St Augustines Place "on the Centre" in mock Tudor buildings the company had occupied since 1896.

ABOVE: Wotton-under-Edge depot in Gloucestershire was the smallest in Bristol Omnibus, from which 45-seat ECW-bodied Bristol MW5G 2970 (982 EHY) is working here. It was new in 1959. GEOFF GOULD

These premises remained in use as an enquiry and booking office, staff canteen, traffic and control office for a further eight years. For decades, the Centre office was among the most distinctive Bristol landmarks with its imposing clock, having originally stood on the city docks quayside until later covered over with the River Frome flowing below: hence its location being termed "on" rather than "at" while the name Centre was derived from the Tramways Centre where the company's network was focused.

I joined direct from school, having stayed on to take O-levels which was a requirement for the job, and then studied for Chartered Institute of Transport examinations which were considered A-level, and then progressing to degree standard. Initially interviewed at Berkeley House, a second interview was held at the Centre offices before

I started in the Bristol Division's traffic department.

The company culture consisted of a distinct hierarchy with each level of management having developed its own status, based on a structure which had evolved from the earliest days. There was, however, contact between managers and all levels, not least because very strong sports and social club associations were in place, which included Bristol Commercial Vehicles.

A tramway tradition revived from 1969 was an illuminated carol bus which toured the streets of Bristol before Christmas, collecting for charities. Similar carol buses followed at Bath, Stroud and Weston-super-Mare, and this was an activity where volunteer staff and managers at every level became involved.

Middle and senior managers were each allocated a company car, with the general manager

having a uniformed chauffeur to deliver him to meetings and functions. With the quality of bus services falling, and the local press constantly running stories about service delays and failures, this risked making managers appear remote from their long suffering passengers and was unhelpful for those staff members having direct contact with the public. To their credit, a few managers made a point of taking bus journeys when the opportunity arose.

A range of measures was in hand to overcome staff shortages, with OMO conversions particularly in urban areas aimed at reducing lost mileage. In Bristol, a permanent complaints office, with two members of staff, recorded daily a high level of lost journeys while also answering phone calls and letters.

The widespread introduction of dual-door Leyland-powered Bristol RELL single-deckers allowed OMO buses with a lively performance to take over from many crew-operated double-deckers. Motorised Setright ticket machines were used for fare collection, with drivers brought into closer contact with passengers – with beneficial results. Not so good, however, was the 44-seat capacity of city RELLs, compared with 70 seats of a Lodekka FLF double-decker, with peak hour passengers unable to find a seat or sometimes travel at all.

Other factors reflecting the times and which deterred some passengers were the high entrance and exit steps of REs compared with the stepless entrances of the Lodekkas they replaced; and with smoking still prevalent, it was no longer possible to segregate this on the top deck, so smokers were asked to sit at the rear of the saloon.

Greater amounts of cream relief was applied to OMO buses from the late 1960s to help the public identify buses with no conductor, which required fare payment on entry. Despite the term OMO, women drivers were also slowly being recruited. Besides having driving instructors across

RIGHT: The smallest ECW-bodied Bristols in the fleet were the 30-seat SUS4A type used where passenger loads were light or clearances were limited. This is 303 (843 THY), new in 1963 and based in the Stroud area. These were powered by a four-cylinder Albion engine. GEOFF GOULD

the Bristol Omnibus area, the company ran a large driving school at Lawrence Hill, with a team of instructors and its own fleet of training buses — and a delegated driving examiner to undertake tests at the conclusion of driving courses.

Radio control

Traffic congestion caused serious disruption to schedules, so some Bristol city buses were fitted with two-way radios to enable inspectors to regulate departures, while also providing security if passengers caused trouble on late-night buses.

This was taken a step farther in the early 1970s with a pioneering Marconi tracking project known as the B-line bus location system being trialled on city routes. Some RELLs had a tracking box fitted at cantrail level above the front nearside wheel. This produced a narrow light beam through a small vertical window, which was reflected from plates attached to lamp posts and bus stops along a route. The plates carried identifying barcodes – long before they became familiar in retailing – and returned a signal to a central control. A display screen showed bus positions along a route and, using

two-way radio, controllers could re-position vehicles if gaps or bunching occurred.

This was said to be the first of its kind in the world and it was monitored closely by NBC. Unfortunately the on-bus equipment was insufficiently robust to withstand jerks and bumps from the road, while its effectiveness was negated by having insufficient spare staff and buses. Improved versions followed and today such tracking is commonplace throughout the transport industry.

Another novel idea to improve bus service control and assistance were Bruin cars. From the late 1960s, police forces around the country introduced panda patrol cars, so named because of their pale blue paintwork with white doors and roof. Bristol police initially employed Morris Minors in this role. Bristol Omnibus adopted something similar to offer high profile patrols by uniformed inspectors.

During 1970, it launched on to the streets of Bristol four Morris Minors painted cream and Tilling green and carrying roof mounted Bristol scroll signs similar to those of the police. Bruin was short for Bristol Urban Inspection. The intention

was that the inspectors could intercept buses, monitor service reliability and offer advice to waiting passengers while remaining in touch by radio to a control room.

High profile they most certainly were, but so similar to the police pandas that they sometimes caused confusion. When replaced four years later, it was with Morris Marina vans in allover green, but retaining large roof signs. Bristol police, meanwhile, had moved on to Ford Escort pandas.

More Marinas, this time red cars with standard company legal lettering, were introduced when Bristol Parkway railway station opened at Stoke Gifford in Gloucestershire in 1972. The cars provided the first UK dial-a-ride service — driven by volunteer, uniformed drivers — to the dismay of taxi drivers who were not permitted to enter the station. The dial-a-ride did not last long, but the station has grown dramatically since, and many more Parkway stations have been established across the country.

OMO double-deckers

Bristol Omnibus was slow to introduce rear-engined double-deckers. This may have been

BELOW: ECW-bodied Bristols in Stroud bus station during the changeover period to NBC livery. An RELL and an MW retain Tilling green and cream, while a Lodekka FLF, two MWs and an RELL are all finished in leaf green and white.
GEOFF GOULD

ABOVE: The
two Bristol VRX
prototypes with
inline offside engines
were the first
vehicles to carry
the double deck
version of OMO
livery but spent a
great deal of time
out of use, as they
were at Lawrence
Hill depot in January
1973 shortly before
they were sold.
C5001 (HHW 933D)
is in front, with the
Scottish Bus Group
destination of C5000
(GGM 431D) partly
visible behind.
MARTIN S CURTIS

diverted to United Automobile and Brighton Hove & District following modification which, ironically, took place in Bristol Omnibus Company's central works.

Two years passed before double-deckers arrived. These were the two prototype VRXs built in 1966 with in-line engine in the offside rear and fitted with 80-seat ECW bodies. They had been on trial with Mansfield District and Central SMT and Bristol Omnibus acquired them for use as OMO buses on city routes. A double-deck version of the cream and green OMO livery was applied, but they were never used without a conductor (their high capacity was probably considered an obstacle) and they spent a great deal of time out of use with mechanical issues. Despite this, I sampled both in service.

To help accelerate the conversion of services to OMO, during the early 1970s the company embarked on a modernisation programme for 15 elderly Bristol LS underfloor-engined single-deckers. Each was completely refurbished over a two-month period with larger engine, updated electrical equipment, fluorescent lighting, new floor and interior trim to similar standards as the latest RELLs. Most were additionally fitted with

partly because of resistance from staff representatives, and arranging for service numbers and destinations on the rear of OMO vehicles was the source of constant difficulties. Even crew-operated Lodekka FLFs began to have their rear displays panelled over to make way for advertising during the 1970s.

Reputedly, one senior manager had said, "The public don't want to know which bus they've just missed", which with so many buses not operating owing to staff shortages was precisely what passengers did want to know in order to decide whether to wait or use an alternative service. I became frustrated by this approach and throughout my career resolved to re-introduce rear route information at every opportunity.

When the Bristol VRT was announced, Bristol Omnibus ordered 28 for delivery in 1968, but then changed the order for the same number of single-deck RELLs. The VRTs were

RIGHT: A Morris
Minor Bruin car
used across the
Bristol area to try
to improve service
reliability, with the
company's Centre
offices behind.
BRISTOL OMNIBUS

LEFT: Cheltenham District Traction Bristol KSW6G 8562 (UHY 375), one of the last of its type in NBC service, in NBC poppy red, but still displaying the Cheltenham coat of arms, together with an advertisement for National Express.
MARTIN S CURTIS

a more modern front panel and windscreen.

While the programme was successful, and demonstrated the abilities of the central works, it was halted after eight buses had been upgraded because the government's 25% bus grant had become available for new vehicles suitable for OMO and it was no longer felt to be expedient to continue. All OMO vehicles were repainted cream and green by late 1972, the last to gain it being a Bristol MW single decker.

Eight 70-seat VRTs arrived in February 1972, and after lengthy negotiation these entered regular service as one-man buses five months later. Like the VR prototypes, they were finished in the double-deck OMO livery. Their dual-door bodywork with centrally positioned stairs and exit door resulted in a cramped and cluttered interior layout. They set the standard for Bristol's city double-deckers for the next ten years.

The double-deck OMO livery offered a more modern image, and after the appearance of the VR prototypes it was decided to try this scheme on a Lodekka FLF with front engine and driver alongside in a separate cab. In May 1971, C7133 was selected but it was soon returned to the works for overhaul, when coincidentally said works was repainting 15 AEC Swifts being transferred from South Wales

Transport to London Country. As an experiment, the green areas of C7133 were also repainted in London Country dark green. It returned to service in this condition and continued in these colours for a considerable period, but remained unique.

New colours and uniforms

With the introduction of NBC's corporate colours in late 1972, all but one part of Bristol Omnibus adopted leaf green, the exception being Cheltenham where the fleet became poppy red. The 36-vehicle strong Cheltenham fleet was repainted within two years, with the claim that this was the first NBC fleet to be entirely in the new colours. Having achieved that,

the first Cheltenham bus was repainted again in January 1975, this time in leaf green with no coat of arms and the remainder of the fleet then followed.

Besides replacing the black-edged gold fleetnames with NBC's white block capitals and double-N symbol (Bristol's until then were scroll fleetnames), some names were shortened, Cheltenham losing District and Bath losing Services. For a variety of reasons, many buses carried the coats of arms of their area. This ceased to be applied in Bath, but remained initially in Cheltenham, Gloucester and Weston.

Branding was more complex in the city of Bristol. Approximately one third of the Bristol Omnibus

BELOW: Freshly repainted in leaf green (including wings and mudguards) and grey wheels, is Gloucester Lodekka LD6G G8509 (963 EHW), new in 1959. The Gloucester coat of arms is also carried, as the one deviation from NBC's standard guidelines.
GEOFF GOULD

RIGHT: While
the first Leyland
Nationals were
driven from the
Cumberland
factory, these 1974
examples (C1441/2:
UAE 993/4N)
arrived in Bristol on
articulated lorries.
This presented the
problem of how to
unload them until a
railway goods yard
was used where a
platform acted as a
ramp. The company's
new head office
building, Berkeley
House, is on the left.
MARTIN S CURTIS

RIGHT: While
the first Leyland
Nationals were
driven from the
Cumberland
factory, these 1974
examples (C1441/2:
UAE 993/4N)
arrived in Bristol on
articulated lorries.
This presented the
problem of how to
unload them until a
railway goods yard
was used where a
platform acted as a
ramp. The company's
new head office
building, Berkeley
House, is on the left.
MARTIN S CURTIS

BELOW: Leyland
Olympian 9505
(JHU 904X) on the
Centre, operating
city route 87 to
Filton Church.
ECW bodied most
Olympians for
NBC, but those for
Bristol and London
Country received
Roe bodywork built
in Leeds. Bristol's
were fitted with
Transign electronic
destination
equipment which
allowed information
to be provided on
both front and
rear. Unreliability
resulted in many
being replaced
by conventional
front "linens", the
Bristol term for
destination blinds.
MSC COLLECTION

fleet formed Bristol Joint Services (identified with a C for City prefix to fleetnumbers). The joint services operation was owned 50% by Bristol Corporation in an arrangement created by the 1937 Bristol Transport Act. Before NBC livery was introduced, these buses had scroll fleetnames with the city arms above, and there was a desire to retain this. The first joint services double-deckers to be painted in NBC green and white retained the gold scroll and arms, as did the RELLs which also retained deep cream lower panels with the new leaf green.

Having several variations was unsatisfactory, but it took time to agree a standard application, during which time various arrangements were mocked up for consideration. Joint services double-deckers began to be painted in NBC green without any fleet markings. It was finally agreed that a smaller, white scroll would be designed and city buses would carry this on their lower panels surmounted by the coat of arms. The NBC symbol was applied in isolation above the driver's cab and the corresponding position on the nearside. Joint services buses thereafter became quite distinct, including on further

new buses, among them a second batch of 20 VRTs.

This was a passing phase, however, as Bristol Joint Services ceased in 1978, with the company taking full ownership of the vehicles and operations. Four years earlier, local government reorganisation had created a new Avon County Council with responsibility for local transport matters.

The new corporate look also extended to staff clothing, and from 1972 drivers' and conductors' black uniforms were gradually superseded by American-style blue-grey designs. This initially included a hook-

on tie, an ill-fitting blouse for both male and female staff and a cap which resembled that of a US police officer. Much of this was rapidly re-thought with a normal jacket soon introduced. Nevertheless, just how smart staff appeared in either old or new styles frequently depended not on the fashion provided, but by each depot's enforcement of staff appearance.

Leyland National

NBC's 50/50 partnership with British Leyland in Bus Manufacturers Holdings determined which vehicles NBC would buy for its subsidiaries. Bristol and ECW met most of the requirement for double-deckers with the VRT and for rural lightweight single-deckers with the LH (Bristol Omnibus bought both), but the standard heavy-duty single-decker was the mass-produced Leyland National which started being built in volume from 1972.

This was a highly standardised product, so operators could no longer specify variations to suit local conditions, and there was immense pressure for NBC subsidiaries to buy them. Many would have preferred to keep buying the Bristol RE or take double-deckers instead, and there was concern in Bristol that there might be insufficient demand for its models to keep Bristol Commercial Vehicles in business. Increased demand for the VRT allayed those fears.

Bristol Omnibus received its first of many Leyland Nationals on December 1, 1972, those initial vehicles going into the joint services fleet. They looked and felt like no other vehicles in the fleet and while contemporary advertising by Leyland suggested the new design would "get 'em back on buses", it was far from obvious how they might achieve this.

First impressions indicated a design that felt austere, with basic seating and finished in unrelieved NBC green. I witnessed a colleague attempt to open the destination box to change the number display, and

Bristol's Greyhound coaching legacy

Bristol Omnibus's extensive coaching activities were branded as Bristol Greyhound. These included private hires, excursions, tours and express services, some of them provided as part of the Associated Motorways network. Its flagship service was the express between Bristol and London.

In 1925, Greyhound Motors of Bristol inaugurated a service between Bristol and London offering through and intermediate fares, which is widely regarded as the world's first express coach operation of its kind. Three years later, Bristol Tramways took control of the Greyhound business and changed the name to Bristol Greyhound.

When NBC was established, Bristol Greyhound coaches carried a cream and signal red livery but in 1970 as one of the first moves to exploit the importance of coach activities in southwest England, all NBC operators in the region adopted revised liveries of white, with a different colour waistband and bold fleetname style. Bristol Greyhound had a magenta band and greyhound logo.

The journey between Bristol and London largely followed the A4 trunk road, with a short section of motorway towards London between Reading and Chiswick. This took around 4hr 45min to complete with a short refreshment break at Marlborough. Completion of the M4 cut this to just 2hr 30min from January 1972 when the company launched its new non-stop service in a blaze of publicity. Suddenly, it became much easier to take a return coach trip to London the same day.

Celebrities were in attendance when the first coach departed from Bristol and three glamorous conductresses (the term used at the time) dressed in magenta and white uniforms distributed publicity in both Bristol and Victoria Coach Station.

Loadings soared, with duplicate coaches and extra services often required. It was one of the reasons why British Rail first introduced its new InterCity 125 High Speed Trains on the competing railway route.

Several changes as a result of NBC influences were beginning to become apparent by then. With management appointments and transfers between what had been two separate groups, new coaches based on Leyland Leopards rather than the Bristol RELH were entering the fleet, despite RELHs continuing to be introduced elsewhere in NBC. As this occurred on Bristol Commercial Vehicles' doorstep, it produced a little local tension.

The Greyhound name disappeared with the advent of the white National coach identity, but both Bristol Omnibus and National Travel went to great lengths to mark the golden jubilee of its original route in 1975, branding it as "50 years of the world's first express coach service".

the handle came away in his hand. Worst of all was the high-pitched clatter of the fixed-head Leyland 510 engine.

Engineers liked them as they were easy to work on and the ergonomically designed cab offered an excellent driving position. Unusually, the gear selector was on the right of the steering wheel and the indicator stalk appeared to come from a Morris Marina car, while other

push-button controls were not as robust as they needed to be. Air-operated pedals were not quite in the same positions as other buses, the accelerator being where the footbrake was on an RE, so drivers had to take care when changing between types. Initially, the lack of anti-roll bars caused passengers concern on cornering and fuel consumption was far from impressive.

LEFT: Bristol Greyhound coaches were cream and signal red when NBC was formed. ECW-bodied Bristol RELH6G coach 2119 (865 UAE), new in 1964, was waiting to depart from Victoria Coach Station in London on an Associated Motorways service to Swindon.
MSC COLLECTION

RIGHT: Completion
of the M4
accelerated journey
times.

BRISTOL LONDON

BRISTOL GREYHOUND

BY MOTORWAY

Bristol Greyhound are racing to give you
faster non-stop services to London as soon as
the motorway is completed in 1972 (scheduled).

Open-top expansion

The Bristol company had
operated open-top double-
deckers along the seafront at
Weston-super-Mare since 1950.

By the time NBC took control,
Lodekkas were performing this
role and more were acquired
from Crosville to expand the
operation. A 1941 K5G new to
Bristol Tramways, GHT 127, was
also brought back from Thomas
Bros of Port Talbot, one of NBC's
smallest subsidiaries.

These were in an established
cream livery but for the 1976
season the Lodekkas (now
including an FLF) each received
a different colour scheme and
name to represent former
tram-operating towns and cities
in the Bristol Omnibus area.
Unfortunately, these failed to
stand out on the long expanses
of beachside roads where
passengers watched for an
approaching bus.

NBC's open-top bus operators
were asked if they wished to
update their fleets with new

Bristol VRT convertible double-
deckers suitable for OMO, but
Bristol Omnibus declined the
offer. These were delivered
elsewhere in NBC during
1977/78. Within a year, Bristol
decided it would after all seek
to run OMO open-toppers, so
a mixed selection of Leyland
Atlanteans and Daimler Fleetlines
was acquired from Hants &
Dorset, Maidstone & District and
Midland Red for conversion and
repaint into the cream livery.

A further open-top Lodekka
had been introduced in Bristol
during 1973 to celebrate the
600th anniversary of Bristol's
Royal Charter. The company's
signwriters painted it into an
elaborate livery with scenes of
the city.

Open-toppers were also
introduced in Bath in 1983 for
city tours, which grew rapidly
into a most successful operation.

Centenary celebrations in 1974

As one of NBC's oldest subsidiaries, and one of the longest established operators in the
country, Bristol Omnibus reached its centenary long before other group companies. This
occurred in 1974. Or was it 1975? The Bristol Tramways Company began operating in
August 1875, but the company marked the occasion a year earlier as it had been formed
in 1874.

Special events included a luncheon attended by the minister of transport, Bristol's
lord mayor, NBC's chairman and other NBC and Bristol Omnibus officials. There was a
centenary bus rally held at the once closely associated aircraft works.

Two hardback publications were produced. The company produced *The People's
Carriage* with contributions from various experts, while I wrote *Bristol – A Century
on the Road*, at a time when such books about a single operator's history were rare.
It was inspired by Ian Allan's *London Bus & Tram Album* but included coverage
of Bristol as both operator and manufacturer, and many of the company's official
photographs.

More double-deckers

Despite the requirement to
purchase Leyland Nationals,
NBC's own studies, and in
particularly its Market Analysis
Project (MAP), identified a need
for a greater proportion of double-
deckers as the company entered
the 1980s.

Large numbers of new VRTs
were delivered, and all 15 in
the London Country fleet, with
highbridge ECW bodies, were
transferred to Bristol. Greater
variety came in 1980 with an
experimental batch of five MCW
Metrobuses with Rolls-Royce
engines, which NBC was anxious
to assess. These were intended for
Bristol city, but staff objections
to their not having dual doors
caused them to be diverted to
Bath where there was no such
resistance.

The VRT's successor was the
Leyland Olympian, also built
initially by Bristol Commercial
Vehicles, and the first of these
arrived in 1982.

Fleet strength by then had fallen
to below 700 as economies were
made and little crew operation
remained. For me, it was time to
leave Bristol Omnibus Company
and move to another NBC
subsidiary. •

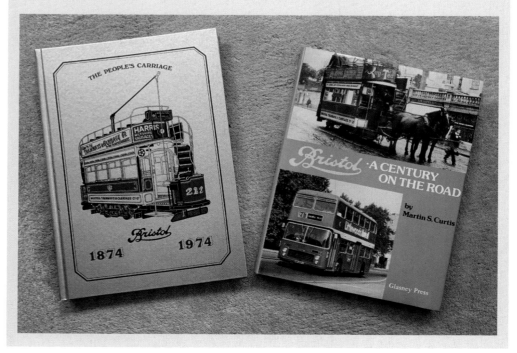

Hants & Dorset

MARK LYONS tells the story of an operator that followed NBC's fashions of successive decades by merging into something larger in the 1970s and then being broken up into smaller units in the 1980s

Hants & Dorset, which by 1972 operated nearly 800 buses and coaches across Hampshire, Dorset and Wiltshire, with some incursions into Berkshire, could trace its roots to the establishment of Bournemouth & District Motor Services in 1916. The British Automobile Traction Company — part of British Electric Traction (BET) — was a significant shareholder.

The fledgling operator struggled to secure suitable vehicles during World War One. Four Straker-Squire chassis were acquired and fitted with charabanc bodies by Bayley's of London. They wore an aluminium livery and carried the fleetname Silver Fleet. The local authority refused to grant it licences to operate public services but in 1918 it acquired two local operators, The Canford

Cliffs Motor Omnibus Company and Eugene Poulain, along with their licences. Postwar expansion added new services and in 1920 it acquired Southampton-based Trade Cars.

The Tilling group acquired a shareholding in 1920 when, in recognition of its enlarged operating area, the company's name was changed to Hants & Dorset Motor Services and it adopted a green livery, which in various shades was to endure for over 50 years. Growth continued through the 1920s by organic expansion and acquisition of other businesses, the operating area by then including much of south Hampshire and south-east Dorset along with services to Salisbury, operated jointly with Wilts & Dorset. It became a publicly quoted company in 1924, was part of the Tilling & BAT grouping from 1928 and was partly railway-owned from

1929 when the Southern Railway acquired 33% of the shares.

Its story became increasingly intertwined with that of Elliott Brothers of Bournemouth, which traded as Royal Blue and operated both coaches and buses. In 1924, Elliott Brothers sold its local bus operations to Hants & Dorset, which in turn agreed not to operate any tours, excursions or long-distance services from Bournemouth.

The two companies opened a new bus station in Bournemouth in March 1931, an impressive two-tier building with entrance on to Exeter Road. Royal Blue coaches used the lower tier and Hants & Dorset buses the upper tier. Hants & Dorset went on to build bus stations in other major towns that it served including Southampton and Winchester.

Tilling purchased the Royal Blue business in 1935 and divided the fleet between Southern

National, Western National and Hants & Dorset. The two National companies retained the Royal Blue brand, which lived on until shortly after the National Bus Company (NBC) introduced its white National brand in 1972. The coaches operated by Hants & Dorset were repainted cream and green.

Hants & Dorset motorbuses replaced part of Poole Corporation's tram system in 1928 and the remainder of that operation in 1935.

BAT influence was apparent in the choice of vehicles in the 1920s and 1930s, which mainly had Leyland chassis. That changed after September 1942 when the Tilling & BAT group was wound up and its subsidiaries divided between BET and Tilling. Hants & Dorset became a Tilling company, and future deliveries of new vehicles were mainly Bristol chassis with ECW bodywork. It became state-owned when Tilling sold its bus operations to the British Transport Commission (BTC) in 1948.

Wilts & Dorset

The first bus to carry the Wilts & Dorset name was operated by one Edwin Coombes who sold his business in autumn of 1914 to Alfred Cannon and Douglas MacKenzie, directors of Worthing Motor Services. They registered

Wilts & Dorset Motor Services in January 1915, with a head office in Amesbury until 1917 when this was moved to Salisbury. The company's name was derived from that of the Wilts & Dorset Banking Company, which Lloyds Bank acquired in 1913.

Coombes became garage manager at Amesbury before he was called up for war service, but was declined re-employment when he was demobbed. He set up another business, Salisbury & District Motor Services, which Wilts & Dorset acquired in 1921, adding to a network of routes it had developed from Salisbury. A new service linked Salisbury with Andover from 1927, and two years later it launched local services in that Hampshire town.

Its first buses were yellow, but the livery changed to red from 1916. In its early years, Wilts & Dorset had close

links with Southdown and was effectively managed from Southdown's Worthing head office. Until it established its own workshops, buses requiring heavy overhaul were sent to Brighton.

It followed Hants & Dorset into the Tilling & BAT grouping in 1931, when the Southern Railway and Tilling obtained shareholdings, and became a Tilling company in 1942. This had the same effect on vehicle choice, moving from Leyland chassis with a variety of bodywork to ECW-bodied Bristols.

World War Two provided growth opportunities for the company, with the rapid expansion of military facilities on Salisbury Plain and the construction of an army camp at Blandford. The fleet, numbering around 100 in 1939, more than doubled in size.

ABOVE: **Hants & Dorset 868 (YEL 227), an ECW-bodied Bristol MW6G coach converted into a one-man-operated service bus, in Gosport in September 1970.**
IAIN MacGREGOR

LEFT: **Hants & Dorset 1117 (5679 EL), an ECW-bodied Bristol Lodekka FS6G new in 1961, in Gosport in May 1972 just before NBC corporate identity began to appear.**
DICK DAPRE

It might have been larger by then had it been possible to agree terms with the Basingstoke-based operator Venture, which had offered itself for sale to Wilts & Dorset in 1933. Venture remained an independent business until March 1945, when the Red & White group acquired it. It was finally placed in the control of Wilts & Dorset after the BTC purchased Red & White in March 1950.

A further significant acquisition was that of Porton Down-based Silver Star in June 1963, a 23-vehicle business that had prospered during the years of National Service, transporting military personnel around the country on weekend leave. Silver Star operated four Leyland Atlanteans, the first rear-engined double-deckers in any of the Transport Holding Company's (THC) Tilling fleets; three were transferred to Bristol Omnibus Company where they were kept for just a year.

A slow merger

A slow merger of Hants & Dorset and Wilts & Dorset began in 1964, when the THC placed Wilts & Dorset under control of Hants & Dorset management. The only outward sign of that change was to the address on the legal lettering of Wilts & Dorset buses.

Two years later, THC acquired United Services Transport which included the coaches of Bournemouth-based Shamrock & Rambler and Charlie's Cars, managing them as part of Hants & Dorset, and four Isle of Wight coach operators acquired in 1967/68 were controlled by Shamrock & Rambler rather than THC's established operator on the island, Southern Vectis. That anomaly was addressed when NBC passed them on to Southern Vectis.

Following delivery of the last Bristol Lodekkas to the sister fleets in 1967, Leyland-engined FLFs with semi-automatic

gearboxes, most new arrivals were ECW-bodied single-deckers on Bristol LH and RE chassis, supplemented in 1967/68 by front-engined Bedford VAMs with bodywork by Strachans and Willowbrook. Unusually for regional company bus operators, most of the single-deckers had dual doors.

Hants & Dorset absorbed Wilts & Dorset in June 1969 and officially became "Hants & Dorset Motor Services trading as Wilts & Dorset". Henceforth, Wilts & Dorset buses were registered in Bournemouth, and a common fleetnumbering system was adopted in October 1971 with vehicles grouped in blocks according to type. Former Wilts & Dorset buses were numbered under 1000 while "native" Hants & Dorset vehicles took similar blocks but in the range 1000 to 1999.

Wilts & Dorset ceased trading in October 1972 and all services were passed to Hants & Dorset. The fleetname was Hants & Dorset, but the colour was Wilts & Dorset's — NBC poppy red rather than leaf

green. Services were renumbered in 1973 to avoid duplication, a process that generally added 200 to the numbers of former Wilts & Dorset services.

Provincial and King Alfred

Hants & Dorset also controlled the Gosport & Fareham Omnibus Company, which traded as Provincial, and which NBC had acquired in 1970. It remained a separate entity owing to the terms of a 1929 Act under which it was established and remained green, its emerald and cream replaced by NBC leaf green and white from 1972.

Until the last were withdrawn in 1973, the Provincial fleet included Guy Arabs that had been heavily rebuilt with Deutz air-cooled engines. NBC drafted in newer vehicles from other fleets to replace some of the oldest inherited buses.

Six Roe-bodied Daimler Fleetlines on order at the time of the takeover were taken into the main Hants & Dorset fleet. They were the first double-deckers suitable for one-man operation.

Six new ECW-bodied Bristol RELLs went to Provincial in their place, setting the scene for future fleet renewal which was 100% single-deck.

Another significant takeover followed in April 1973 when Hants & Dorset acquired Winchester-based operator King Alfred Motor Services, a fleet made up mainly of Leylands and AECs, but also three nearly new Metro-Scania single-deckers which were transferred to join the only other examples of that type in NBC service, at London Country; three early production Leyland Nationals came in exchange.

As part of a tidying up of NBC companies' operating areas, the Swanage operation of Western National was transferred to Hants & Dorset in 1974. The Shamrock & Rambler coach business passed to National Travel South West the same year, but returned to Hants & Dorset in 1981.

NBC also addressed the high average age of the Hants & Dorset fleet — and facilitated an increase in one-man operation — by transferring 39 rear-engined

Leylands from Maidstone & District, a former BET company. Thirty-three Panther single-deckers with Willowbrook bodies arrived in 1972, followed in 1973 by six Atlantean double-deckers dating from 1959-61 with Metro-Cammell bodies. Only five of the Atlanteans went into service and they were moved on to Western National (including Devon General) in 1976.

Most new buses in the 1970s were standard NBC types — Leyland Nationals and ECW-bodied Bristol VRs and LHs — but there also were 30 front-engined Ford R1014s, 25 with ECW bodywork in 1974 and five with Plaxton Derwent bodies two years later.

Break up and privatisation

The Hants & Dorset name became dormant in April 1983 (the business was dissolved in 1990) when the company was one of the first across NBC's southern region to be split into smaller, locally focused units. Five new companies took the place of the relative monolith built up between 1964 and 1972.

ABOVE: The rebuilt Guy Arabs in the Provincial fleet included 62 (HAA 771E), based on a 1944 Arab II chassis new to United Welsh, which had a Deutz air-cooled engine installed and new Reading body built in 1967. It was still in NBC service in Gosport in May 1972.
DICK DAPRE

Hampshire Bus Company, with head office in Eastleigh and retaining the poppy red livery, took over the operations in Basingstoke, Winchester and Southampton. Wilts & Dorset Bus Company, with office in Poole and also remaining poppy red, covered Bournemouth, Poole, Lymington and Salisbury, a significantly different operating area from the old company. Provincial Bus Company merged Hants & Dorset's Fareham operations with those of Gosport & Fareham and painted its buses leaf green.

Shamrock & Rambler Coaches, which took over some of Hants & Dorset's private hire and coaching operations, had its offices and depot in Bournemouth. The coach operations based in Southampton were transferred to another subsidiary, Pilgrim Coaches, in January 1984. The central works at Barton Park, Eastleigh, which had replaced the previous facility in Southampton in 1982, became Hants & Dorset Engineering.

The five businesses passed to new buyers between February and July 1987, following the government's decision that NBC should be privatised and its subsidiaries sold off individually. First to go, that February, was the engineering business. Hants & Dorset Engineering had ceased trading in 1986 but part of the operation was reborn as Hants & Dorset Distribution, which was acquired by property developer Robert Beattie's Frontsource venture along with other NBC engineering companies. Former Hants & Dorset Engineering employee Peter Drew established vehicle refurbishment business

appeared on the legal lettering of buses it did not feature in fleetnames or other publicity. Go-Ahead Group acquired Wilts & Dorset in August 2003. It became the foundation stone of Go South Coast and went on to drop the traditional name, their place taken by local brands Morebus (Poole and Bournemouth), Salisbury Reds and Purbeck Breezers.

The last to be sold, that July, was Shamrock & Rambler. Its new owner was Drawlane, which acquired three larger NBC companies in 1988 and went on to buy several others from their management buy-out teams. Drawlane was later reformed as British Bus and formed a major part in what today is Arriva. Shamrock & Rambler missed out on that. It closed in April 1989 following the loss of National Express contracts.

Although the historic company names have all disappeared from daily life, Go South Coast respects its heritage. It painted two double-deckers into historic Wilts & Dorset liveries (one Tilling red and cream, the other in prewar red and grey) to mark the operator's centenary in 2015 and painted another the following year in Tilling green and cream Hants & Dorset livery to mark 100 years since that company was established. All three vehicles are still so adorned in 2022. •

BELOW: Go South Coast 1019 (YN06 JWW), an East Lancs-bodied Scania OmniDekka in prewar Wilts & Dorset livery applied in 2015 to mark that company's centenary.
MARK LYONS

Hants & Dorset Trim, which is based today at Eastleigh and forms part of Go-Ahead Group's Go South Coast business.

Hampshire Bus became the first NBC subsidiary to be bought by Stagecoach, that April, along with the small Pilgrim Coaches operation. It sold all the Southampton area operations six months later to Solent Blue Line, then part of the privatised Southern Vectis and today another part of Go South Coast. The remainder of Hampshire Bus today is a major component of Stagecoach South.

Provincial became the first of just two NBC subsidiaries to be sold to its employees (Luton & District was the other), acquired that May through an employee share ownership plan. In recognition of this status, it traded as People's Provincial and revived its traditional emerald green livery. FirstBus acquired the company in 1995 and it now forms part of First Hampshire & Dorset.

Wilts & Dorset's management bought that company in June 1987. Among businesses it went on to acquire, in 1993, was Blandford-based Damory Coaches for which it registered a new company called Hants & Dorset Motor Services. Although the title

Speaking up for the
workers

JAMES FREEMAN renews contact with a former NBC driver who has devoted much of his life to improving working conditions for his colleagues

Trades unions played an essential part in representing employees' interests in the state-owned bus companies, as indeed they continue to do with their private sector successors today. While this may often only attract public attention at times of disagreement when disputes disrupt services, union representatives and managers are in regular contact on matters small and large that generally keep the wheels turning.

Let me introduce you to one of those many representatives who I met again last year, when I moved back to Winchester where I had cut my teeth as an 18-year-old bus conductor when I

was just 18 in 1974, working for Hants & Dorset Motor Services. I have been driving a couple of days a week with what is now Stagecoach in Winchester and the one person left at Winchester

depot still working there from when I did my first stint there is Nick Knight, these days a spritely 73-year-old.

Although already a "one-man" driver, he occasionally worked overtime on the crew double-deckers. One night he was working with me and I persuaded the depot inspector to let us take ex-King Alfred Park Royal-bodied AEC Renown 2212 (596 LCG) in place of the usual Lodekka on the 20:10 service 48 to Southampton – a 3hr round trip via Fair Oak and Eastleigh. Nick, then 27, was ready to have a go.

What he did not know, until we set off, was that 2212 only had two working gears — first and fourth, bottom and top — on its semi-automatic transmission. He soldiered on and remembers it to this day.

He also still drives for Stagecoach and does a great deal more besides. On May 1, 2022, he celebrated 50 years since he first joined Hants & Dorset as a conductor. Few today manage to

make almost their whole career in one industry, let alone one place, but Nick is one and his is a wonderful tale to tell.

"I like driving buses", he says, "that's the core of it." But Nick has used his interest and enjoyment to do much more with his career than simply drive. Mention the fact that he has been an officer of what used to be the National Union of Railwaymen (NUR) and is now the RMT for most of that time and you start to see where this is going.

He has dedicated his life to serving others. Fundamentally, driving buses is a vital service for local people, but Nick took it farther, using his abilities to help his fellow workers and still today sits as a lay member on employment tribunals, often taking on cases that last many days in court. He is the model of a modern trade unionist, for he does not shout and wave his arms about, yet over the years has worked effectively to improve the lot of his fellow workers, using his charm and skill and, increasingly, experience to make change happen in the best possible way.

"Our power was in persuasion," he says. "I can remember saying that the company is like a wife: you may not always agree with them, but you have to live with them."

Lure of the railways

It might have been different, had Nick been born a decade earlier, for as he says "the love of my life was the railways and I dreamed of being an engine driver". He joined British Rail, aged 21, in 1969. He was told that Salisbury was the place to go, where they were crying out for second men. "We worked on the Exeter-Salisbury-Waterloo line, as well as the Portsmouth-Salisbury-Cardiff service and the stone trains from Frome Quarry up to Woking. I loved it." But it did not work out and he ended up working for a spot-welding business in Alresford.

Nick was an Andover lad, born in December 1948 to school teacher parents and the third child of four. When he left Andover Secondary Modern school in 1964, he took up an apprenticeship with the old-established Andover firm of Watson & Haig, which survived to be bought out in the 1990s. After moving round the departments he settled down in the blacksmith's shop.

He did well, buying his first car, an Austin Somerset that cost him £50, at the age of 17, but he had itchy feet and joined Wilts & Dorset as a fitter/improver at its Amesbury depot. He enjoyed it and got behind the wheel of buses when moving them round the depot. This gave him some good early insights into the bus business, but there was talk of redundancies and he yearned to join the railways, hence the move to Salisbury in 1969 and ending up in Alresford.

ABOVE: At the time Nick Knight was starting out as a one-man driver, Hants & Dorset was reducing its dependence on conductors by NBC transferring Leyland Panthers like Willowbrook-bodied 1694 (JKK 189E) from Maidstone & District.
MARK HAMPSON

LEFT: Back behind the wheel of Renown 2212, remembering the night when it only had two working gears.
JAMES FREEMAN

In 1972, he and his first wife Karen found a flat in Winchester – a double-storey property over a shop in the High Street. The marriage did not last, but Nick stayed there until 1977, round the corner from the bus station.

He needed a job. A friend was a bus conductor and Nick thought that might work for him, too. At this time, in 1972, there were still two operators in Winchester, King Alfred Motor Services with its base in the St John's Rooms on the Broadway and Hants & Dorset round the corner in the bus station.

Nick went to King Alfred first, but he did not get a positive response. Walking up Buskin Lane, he looked up into the Hants & Dorset canteen. "I could see them playing snooker and it looked a good place," he says. "I went and saw the chief inspector, Ernie Eames, and shortly after I was sitting in my best suit in front of the operating superintendent, SAH "Sam" Marsh whose real name was Seth, a tall and initially somewhat forbidding man."

Nick takes up the story: "To my surprise, he said 'We've got no work for you' and I went home, rather deflated. The following day Karen told me there was a gentleman in a dark blue uniform to see me. It was Earnie Eames again to say Mr Marsh would like to see me. I think he had been in touch with the railway at Salisbury and got good reports. He offered me a coffee and asked when I could start. My employment as a conductor began on May 1, 1972. Strangely enough I later found that I got on very well with Mr Marsh."

Nick's can-do approach nearly got him into trouble during those early months as a conductor. One evening there was a shortage of fuelling/shunting staff in the bus station and Pete Ayling, the fueller, was getting a backlog of buses queuing out into Friarsgate. Nick was late spare conductor, so Pete asked for some help and Nick assisted in shunting the yard all evening, which solved the problem nicely.

But the following morning, all hell broke loose as it was

realised that Nick (a conductor without a PSV licence) had been driving the buses round. He was at serious risk of the sack and was summoned to see Mr Marsh who asked where he had learned to drive a bus. At Amesbury, of course. Mr Marsh, showing his common sense, told Nick: "We'll take it in good faith" and sent him to the Hants & Dorset driving school in Southampton, where he passed his test at the age of 23 on December 14, 1972.

Union involvement

Nick soon became a "one-man-operator" (no women drivers then, though that was all about to change), driving and collecting fares, which was still new then. He has enjoyed that aspect of the job ever since. But satisfying as the driving was, there was to be a crucial and important extra dimension to his career, as he started to get involved with the busmen's union which, because Hants & Dorset had once been owned by the Southern Railway, was the NUR.

Frank Jackson, a driver who lived in Winnall but hailed from Blackpool, was the branch chair at Winchester depot. Nick started to attend branch meetings and quickly realised that they needed somebody to take the minutes and write them up. By 1973 he was branch secretary, initially for six months, but he kept the job for 46 years, stepping down at the end of 2019.

Nick was involved in representing staff members at disciplinary meetings and

in the annual round of wage negotiations. If done properly, the role can make a real difference to union members. Always fair-minded, Nick would stand up for his members but not defend the indefensible. He learned how to negotiate with managers to get the best outcomes – his style being to see how best to work together to achieve what he needed. He also learned how easy it was to deflect the conversation to achieve what he wanted.

His common sense and interest in doing things properly propelled him on to the Hants & Dorset NUR Central Committee, consisting of branches from Winchester, Poole, Bournemouth, Ringwood, Lymington, Southampton, Eastleigh,

Fareham, Basingstoke, Andover, Salisbury and Pewsey. "At first I was unpopular because I was anti-strike. In my experience there are two kinds of trade unionists, those who want a fight and the others who get out their slide-rules. Our power was in persuasion and we did some good deals," he says.

Employment tribunals

By 1980, Nick was looking to develop his union career. At first he had the idea of being a full-time paid divisional organiser. It looked like good money and he sat an exam, getting an excellent result, but when he realised it was a five-year fixed term contract he decided to stay as a bus driver. Almost straight away, though, another opportunity opened up.

The government of the day was seeking nominations for people to sit on employment tribunals from the trade unions on the one side and Confederation of British Industry (CBI) on the other. He applied. "You had to have been a branch secretary for at least eight years and I had to go before the senior employment tribunal judge on the Southampton circuit, to check for neutrality. I got selected and have been sitting as a lay member (there would be a chair and two lay members) ever since."

Back in 1981 Nick was one of the youngest tribunal members, at just 33. Today he is one of the oldest, having sat on and off for 40 years, working around his bus driving and branch duties. "I love it more than anything," he says. •

ABOVE: Renown 2212, restored to how it looked after Hants & Dorset bought the King Alfred business, at a running day in May 2019. NEIL GOW

Maidstone & District

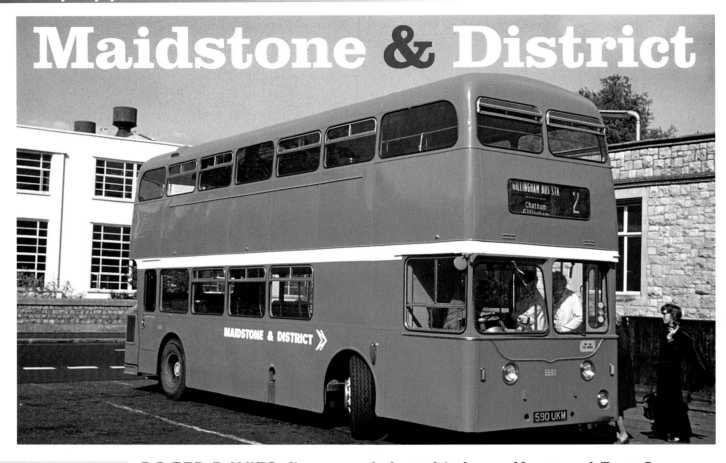

ROGER DAVIES discovered that this large Kent and East Sussex operator was more about urban services than hop gardens and apple orchards — and it was in the forefront of the commuter coach boom into London in the 1980s

Maidstone & District Motor Services (M&D) was one of the BET group companies sold into state ownership in May 1968, nine months before the National Bus Company (NBC) came into being. It was established on March 22, 1911 and based in Knightrider House, Maidstone which once was home to Roy Plomley, creator of the radio show *Desert Island Discs*. Its fleet of almost 800 ran out of 18 depots across west Kent and east Sussex.

It exuded an image, promoted through its publicity, of stately dark green buses ambling through hop gardens and apple orchards. To distant folk like me, it was impossible to understand why it owned so many double-deckers.

Initially, NBC influence was behind the scenes. Amalgamating two groups, it found it often had

two or three depots in quite small towns and large head offices quite close to each other. A process of amalgamation started and while M&D and neighbouring East Kent were both ex-BET, also were affected. Some operation swaps and depot closures took place, M&D losing its Ashford operations to East Kent, while its Hastings, Rye and Faversham operations moved the other way.

An effect of this policy was of alien buses appearing in fleets, like M&D Leyland Atlanteans joining the AECs at East Kent. London Country expanded beyond the old London Transport boundaries and began to take over M&D routes in Gravesend, with the M&D depot at Overcliffe finally closing. In 1978, the people on the huge Valley Drive estate must have wondered what NBC was up to, as after 17 years of the likes of Atlanteans and other modern types they had open platform Routemasters foist upon them.

The most significant change was the amalgamation of head office functions into the large 1960s office block of East Kent at Station Road, west Canterbury and M&D buses gained this address on their legal lettering. Thankfully, NBC did not make the error of combing the fleets, both staying green or red and keeping their names. It is true that at a dinner party in Maidstone the name Northdown was suggested and even a blue livery, but we were spared that.

Some functions remained at Knightrider House, but structural problems with the building made a move sensible. The M&D schedules office flatly refused to move east and was accommodated above the offices in the adjoining bus station and the operating depot remained.

Vehicle purchases
At first bus deliveries were unchanged. After a flirtation

with rear-engined single-deckers, Leyland Panthers and Daimler Fleetlines, M&D reverted to short 45-seat mid-engined Leyland Leopards, building up a fleet of 75.

NBC influence was first felt in 1972 when the last of the Leopards arrived in leaf green but more striking, and rather encouragingly, 20 MCW-bodied Atlantean PDR1A/1 Specials, precursors of the AN68 and much better than the early types, were diverted from Midland Red. These hugely popular buses spent their lives at Gillingham depot, were jealously guarded and were the first new double-deckers to arrive in corporate leaf green.

Another NBC-inspired move that year involved the exchange with Northern General of 12 single-deck Fleetlines for 12 Alexander-bodied double-deck Fleetlines. Despite a large successful collection of the double-deck variety, M&D never got on with the single-deck version. This may be to do with them being dual door. Most operators flirted with such things at the time but soon reverted to much safer single-door vehicles.

NBC vehicle policy soon began to influence. It only received 81 new Leyland Nationals plus some secondhand. A significant number was disposed of after only short lives, particularly the least useful 41-seaters. Why M&D bought these after the small Leopards is a puzzle to me, as is the subsequent purchase of 43-seat Fords R1014s. All were a pain to allocate.

The Bristol VRT started to arrive in profusion. The first were the very lowheight 13ft 5in version to fit under Sackville arch in Bexhill. Next up were mid-range 13ft 8in ones, followed in 1975 by 15 VRT2s with highbridge 14ft 6in bodies. M&D decided these gave a much better environment for customers and crews and ordered more, this time VRT3s. In 1978, it discovered that the 13ft 8in version was the cheapest of the three, so given our parlous financial state we reverted to those midway through an order for 25.

Express and tour coaches became the responsibility of NBC's Central Activities Group.

Much more excitement came in 1975, when M&D was chosen to be NBC's testbed for the new generation of double-deckers and took in five each of the Scania/

MCW Metropolitan and the front-engined Volvo Ailsa with Alexander body. They were to be pitted against four VRT3s, two each with Gardner 6LXB and Leyland 501 engines, and off the 14 popped to Hastings.

NBC influence also came into interiors and we entered the orange plastic phase. We all understood the need for economy in those dark days, but did it have to look so cheap? The later moquette was much better.

In 1976, the busy town centre stops in Military Road, Chatham were replaced by a purpose built bus station in the new Pentagon shopping mall. This had unique features and problems. To the outsider, a consequence was the application of large fleetnumbers on the front dome for the closed-circuit television cameras. I added the rear ones when inspectors — confined out of sight in a control room — pointed out that it was as useful to see what buses were leaving as well as those arriving. The Pentagon is a story in itself. Suffice it to say that NBC was keen to be associated with its launch, but was conspicuously absent as we strove to sort out its myriad problems.

Viewed from inside
On March 1, 1977 I arrived as area manager north west with M&D based at the by then largely empty Luton Road offices. At the

same time the trial buses moved there too.

I received a few initial sharp shocks. First, my impression of M&D was totally wrong. Serving the Medway Towns with a population of a quarter of a million and the over 100,000 population areas of greater Maidstone where M&D was the majority operator, Tunbridge Wells and Tonbridge, and Hastings and Bexhill, the thing was practically a municipal operator. No wonder it needed so many double-deckers. There were busy interurban routes largely unchallenged by trains that headed for London.

They did wander through hops and apples, but that was not what it was all about. In Medway, we ran high frequency busy services in heavy traffic and climbing some of the fiercest hills I had seen, the "Kent Alps". I had come from Cumbria and Sheffield. Boy did those buses work. I also realised that M&D was a hugely strong local brand largely well thought of.

It was not quite the same internally. M&D was viewed at

Canterbury head office as a rather unwanted green appendage to the west. I soon realised that, as long I delivered, everyone there was quite happy to let me get on with it, and with my own schedules office in Maidstone, I virtually had my own 340-strong bus company. But delivering that had its challenges.

Customer numbers were falling through the floor for all the post-World War Two changes in lifestyle we know about. Costs were rising and fares shot up to eye-watering levels. NBC had been told by government not to change services until the new county councils set up in 1974 made up their minds what they wanted under their new coordinating role, so losses continued to mount. Finally in 1977 we were able to take action but it was pretty brutal, as our finances were in a dire state and we had to meet NBC's government-stipulated financial commitments.

It was a painful process. Over those few years, I shut three depots, downgraded another and made 366 redundancies. But it worked and things began to improve financially, although not for the once large coach fleet that dwindled as holiday habits changed

NBC was still happy for us to carry on testing new bus types over the Chatham hills and

in 1980 we took in five MCW Metrobuses of three different types and six Willowbrook-bodied Dennis Dominator. Five promised Leyland Titans never appeared.

The Dominators gave rise to an interesting NBC-related tale. In 1985, the tall ships race came to Chatham and we needed to hire some double-deckers. We tried throughout NBC but nobody had any to spare. I had seen in *Buses* that Stevensons of Uttoxeter wanted rid of the Dominators it had acquired from East Staffordshire Council (which now part-owned Stevensons), so we hired four. They turned out to be in excellent condition, so we offered to buy its whole fleet of Dominators. There was some curious shuffling about and

finally we were told we could only have nine and had to hand back some we had on loan. The rest went to Thamesdown Transport in Swindon.

It was only many years later, talking to Thamesdown managing director John Owen, that I discovered municipal operators had an agreement to offer roadworthy buses for sale to all other municipals before selling to NBC. Despite some arriving with Stevensons legal lettering, the deal was done with East Staffs. All this activity gave us possibly the most varied and interesting NBC fleet.

The birth of Invictaway
During 1978, in the parish council-owned windmill in

Meopham, I was holding a traffic meeting away from phones. My Sheerness superintendent, George Digby, said it was silly that to go to London you only needed to go to a station and hop on a train while to use the limited service we provided for National Express you had to book three days in advance. What was needed was a pay-as-you-enter coach service.

Brilliant, I thought, and we set to work beefing up the service and calling it Invictaway. This referred to the Invicta symbol of Kent, not going into Victoria Coach Station. As was the custom, it was raised at a regular liaison meeting with British Rail, remember two state-owned organisations. The railway people said, "London is ours, we'll object and win, so get lost". Invictaway was gone but not forgotten.

A bit of a foretaste and proof it would work came when we took over Green Line route 719 to Wrotham and extended it to Maidstone and Tenterden, renumbering it 919, something NBC could do that London Transport could not.

Then along came the Transport Act 1980, deregulating coach services on which the shortest possible journey was 30miles. It also removed British Rail's effective veto over new services that it saw as a commercial threat.

NBC became increasingly concerned by the public claims being made by British Coachways, a consortium of independent operators that was planning to establish a rival nationwide service, and set about reforming National Express, ultimately very successfully. It was also concerned about the plans for commuter coaches into big cities, particularly London. Not only would this affect National Express, but it felt that NBC should have a share of the market.

After a regional traffic meeting, I received a call at home from my traffic manager, David Rabey. "We're doing Invictaway from October 6 when the new Act comes in," he announced. We set to, dusted off the old plans, but this was a new ball game so we added more commuter runs. Unions were hugely supportive. After a decade of service cuts, depot closures, redundancies and fare increases, here was something positive. The

physiological effect of Invictaway cannot be overstated

A key part of the Act was the change in the burden of proof. Objectors now had to prove their case. As Invictaway was always licensed and not notified, British Rail could have objected but with everything else going on it stood no chance, as I told them when I rang to say we were doing it. Many years later a senior rail man told me, "We didn't really mind, you took the standing passengers."

As planned, Invictaway was launched on October 6, 1980. The mayor of Gillingham cut a ribbon and we wore Invictaway teeshirts, which was quite a feat, as customising teeshirts was not common then. In a nice act of support, our general manager, Bill Jelpke, had a meeting in London and got off the train at Gillingham to take the coach.

And then it took off. None of us was prepared for how the market skyrocketed. You could put a coach on one day and it was full the next. It was astonishing.

It was easy to see why the coaches were umpteen times better than the train, They gave a door-to-door service, offering comparable journey times and incidentally reducing car traffic going to railway stations. They gave a personal service with regular drivers and customers, were cheaper but best of all there was a guaranteed seat. We were the only ones to offer an offpeak service running until 23:15 and this proved hugely popular for many of the same reasons. Soon we were running every half hour from Medway during the day, the highest service level ever.

The end of Olsen
In early 1982, the largest commuter coach operator, Olsen of Strood, ceased operating overnight. The next morning we grabbed anything we could and went around Olsen routes with management on board, including me, assuring them we would bring them home and honour their tickets. An effect of this was the entry into the market of The Kings Ferry which was later to do so much on vehicle quality.

There was a lengthy rail strike in the summer of 1982, for part of which I was on holiday in Lanzarote and broke a habit by looking at UK newspapers. I would return to the pool content, saying, "They're still out". Many of those coming to us never returned to trains. We also expanded that year into Maidstone and, less successfully, Tunbridge Wells.

With surging loads, our minds turned to double-deckers and we converted three of the PDR1A/1 Atlanteans to dual purpose with upgraded axles. We had adopted a black and red image for publicity, bus stops and the advertisements on London Underground and had not been able to resist putting it

BELOW: **One of the three Duple Dominant-bodied Leyland Leopards painted in the black Invictaway livery, 2152 (BKJ 152T), waiting in London about to undertake a commuter run to Rainham in May 1983.** HARRY HAY/THE BUS ARCHIVE

on three Leopards as well. The three Atlanteans had it too and looked very impressive and were often to be found with full loads during the off peak.

Then NBC came up trumps with the Leyland Olympian coach. We took five in 1983 and ended up with 14. Their appearance is a matter of taste, but once you had ridden in one with that huge front window upstairs and the nicely appointed interior, you tended to be smitten. I think with these we can claim to have started the increase in vehicle quality.

NBC suddenly decreed that all such services be branded Green Line and painted in that livery. We said Green Line meant nothing in our patch, but Invictaway was a huge brand. As a sop, we painted one coach, 2421, into that layout then ignored it.

The whole thing demonstrated NBC willing to rise to a challenge

and meeting what turned out to be a huge customer demand. It was one of the most successful and rewarding things I was ever involved in.

Devolved and privatised

The head office and management structure devised in the early 1970s when M&D and East Kent had 1,200 buses was inappropriate by the 1980s when we had 700. NBC's southern region was steadily splitting its companies into smaller units and our turn came on May 22, 1983. Early that year, all managers from my level up and all head office staff were fired and given the chance to apply for new jobs, of which there were fewer, in the four new companies, East Kent, M&D, Hasting & District and Kent Engineering

I became traffic manager of M&D and the new head office was to be

at Luton Road where my colleague David Powell, now fleet engineer, and I had existed in splendid isolation for several years. We had to convert it into a head office, which we managed on time. Some staff transferred back but we took on quite a few new ones. I always remember Luton Road head office as a happy and pleasant place to be. All looked set fair.

It was not to be. In the summer of 1984 I sat in my garden and read the draft of what became the Transport Act 1985. Everything I had known was changing, M&D, along with all of NBC, was to be sold and the market completely changed. NBC was keen to be privatised and shake off the dead hand of state ownership but as a whole like British Telecom and British Airways. That was not what transport secretary Nicholas Ridley wanted. When NBC's final suggestion — splitting

it into three groups of non-contiguous companies — was rejected by being thrown in the bin, we knew the game was up. It became 70 famous names for sale which was neat unless you worked for one.

Had NBC succeeded there would no doubt have been guidance on how to deal with deregulation, the competition authorities who were now let loose on us and other issues. As it was, we were very much on our own to sort it out.

To bring some stability we put in a bid to buy the company, announced on March 21, 1986 near the 75th anniversary, and this led us into all sorts of things like setting up a pension scheme. Our relationship with NBC became largely one of vendor and potential purchaser. We still had to do what it told us like showing around other potential purchasers, which was challenging.

For deregulation, I regarded it as a clean sheet of paper and went for simple high frequency services in urban areas, of which we had a lot, publicised by frequency, so folk did not usually need a timetable. It meant reprinting all timetables but we had plenty of time from February when all registrations had to be made, until October 26. Changes were allowed in that time and I introduced my first minibuses in July and September.

It meant we could rebrand everything at one go including buildings and buses, although we had started introducing new fleetnames and cream trim. There were no other bids for the company and the change of ownership was scheduled for October 26, with the sale meeting a few days prior. At the last moment it was put back until November 7, but it was too late to stop the rebranding. If you have a picture of an M&D bus between October 26 and November 7, 1986 it is in privatisation identity but still state-owned.

At 13:55 on November 7, NBC got our money we got a bus company and it was the parting of the ways, poignant as some of us were NBC products. But it was the start of the management buyout years that were I think the most exciting and interesting parts of the M&D story. It changed hands again, on April 13, 1995, when British Bus bought the company. Today it is part of Arriva Southern Counties. •

BELOW: The last buses ordered by NBC for M&D were 39 Mercedes-Benz L608D minibuses appropriately converted by Rootes of Maidstone. This May 1987 view of 1024 (D24 KKP) in Tonbridge in May 1987 shows the M&D logos that covered the NBC double-N. ROY MARSHALL/THE BUS ARCHIVE

Western National & Southern National

The state-owned operators covering Cornwall, Devon, Somerset and Dorset were merged in 1969, only to be split into smaller units 13 years later. MARTIN S CURTIS explains what this meant for one part of the business.

The Western National Omnibus Company, another Tilling concern, was the operator associated most closely with the Bristol company, so it came as a surprise to me, on transferring there from Bristol in the early 1980s, that there were several structural and cultural differences between the two organisations.

Western National covered a vast area of south-west England and from late 1969 had formally absorbed its sister company, the Southern National Omnibus Company. They had previously been managed from the same head office — National House, Queen Street, Exeter — with a common management board and a combined fleet numbering system. The company names reflected the territories of the former Great Western and Southern Railways rather than

where the buses ran. Some Southern National routes ran to the west of some of Western National's.

The fleet of slightly below 1,000 vehicles included coaches on the extensive Royal Blue network, subsumed subsequently into National Express. The bus operations were intermingled with those of former BET company Devon General, which NBC placed under Western National control following Devon General's acquisition of Exeter Corporation's bus services in 1970. Nevertheless, there remained areas of the West Country where the company's services were detached, with no direct bus connections to other parts of the network.

The company culture was formal, with managers and staff often being addressed by their title and surnames, yet senior officials took a close interest in their managers, who were

dispersed many miles from Exeter. The entire fleet wore the appropriate corporate styles, buildings were adorned with NATIONAL lettering and staff uniforms were of group style, although the issue of clothing was less thorough than other NBC subsidiaries. In view of the company's history, however, the National name came naturally to its staff and the public at large.

A drive to convert almost all services to one-man operation was well underway, despite reservations about converting the relatively few urban or busy services requiring double-deckers. This was being accelerated by the transfer of elderly vehicles, suitable for use without conductors, from distant fleets elsewhere in NBC.

Competition to Portland
When I arrived at my new base in Weymouth, among the first issues to contend with was competition

**LEFT: Competition
from Smiths of
Portland in July
1985. MAR 517L, a
12-year-old Bedford
YRT with Plaxton
Elite Express
body, was loading
in Weymouth.**
IAIN MacGREGOR

on the route to Portland. This was before deregulation occurred, so it was rare for two operators to face head-to-head rivalry. Smiths of Portland had become established on this important corridor owing to what appeared to be a licensing error, and this culminated in a public inquiry attended by groups of rival public supporters from Portland and Weymouth. Eventually, an agreement was established allowing the two operators to cover slightly different routes on the Isle of Portland.

Because of the company's railway heritage, Western National road staff were members of the National Union of Railwaymen (NUR) rather than the more usual Transport & General Workers Union (TGWU). Nearby were other NUR branches covering British Rail, National Carriers and Sealink, but there was little coordination between them.

Coach activities in the West Country had long formed a significant part of the companies' activities. What had once been the Royal Blue express service network was now increasingly drawn into the National Express network and was further being transformed by the growing motorway system and upgrading of trunk roads, some of which became dual carriageways. This

process was slower in Western National's area than many other parts of the country.

A market for excursions and tours continued, ranging from all-day excursions to evening drives, and with local booking offices still in existence, a small team of staff was fully occupied meeting this demand.

Transfer of passengers between Weymouth railway station and the Sealink terminal at Weymouth Quay brought brief but large crowds of people making these connections, some of whom made the journey by a Sealink-liveried Leyland National towing an ex-BEA/British Airways luggage trailer, previously hauled by Routemasters between central London and Heathrow.

Yet another seaside activity was the limited provision of open-

top bus travel, achieved by the temporary transfer each summer of a vehicle from Devon General. It retained NBC poppy red and white livery, but the fleetname and vehicle name was changed to fit its Dorset location. This had generally been a Leyland Atlantean, but in 1982 a Bristol VRT arrived with staff initially refusing to drive it.

That was because, by agreement with Weymouth staff, double-deckers without power steering were confined to school services or contracts such as to the Winfrith Atomic Energy Establishment, rather than all-day services. The arrival of a Devon General VRT with a low (three-digit) fleetnumber led to the assumption by the local staff representatives that it must lack power steering.

**BELOW: Leyland
National 2823
(MOD 823P) and
ex-British Airways
trailer T2 in Sealink
livery, operating
the transfer service
between Weymouth
railway station and
Weymouth Quay.**
MARTIN S CURTIS

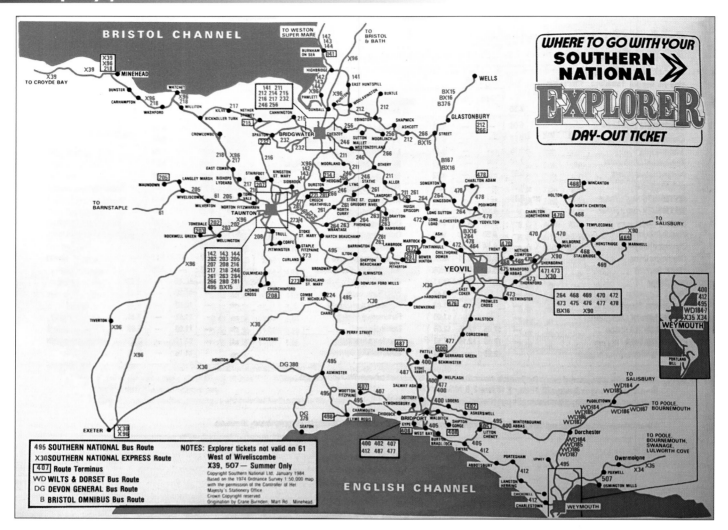

Legend:

495 SOUTHERN NATIONAL Bus Route
X30 SOUTHERN NATIONAL EXPRESS Route
407 Route Terminus
WD WILTS & DORSET Bus Route
DG DEVON GENERAL Bus Route
B BRISTOL OMNIBUS Bus Route

NOTES: Explorer tickets not valid on 61
West of Wiveliscombe
X39, 507 — Summer Only

Copyright Southern National Ltd. January 1984
Based on the 1974 Ordnance Survey 1:50,000 map
with the permission of the Controller of Her
Majesty's Stationery Office
Crown Copyright reserved
Origination by Crane Burnden; Mart Rd. Minehead.

ABOVE: Network map of the new Southern National company.

I solved that one by jumping in the cab and taking the bus around the block to demonstrate this was not the case. That caused astonishment, as previously most managers had been promoted through the clerical ranks, and staff had no idea that somebody at my grade was able to drive a bus. It was a practice I applied again from time to time, as other issues with vehicles arose.

Local decisions

NBC invested heavily in training for its managers, which often involved colleagues from a wide range of subsidiaries attending residential courses. By meeting and sharing knowledge with fellow managers and training covering all aspects of the business, these courses contributed greatly to the professionalism of NBC's managers. Such career development has been largely lost in the bus industry today.

On one such three-week course at Chelmsford in 1982, there was

much speculation about how many subsidiaries would follow Western National in being broken up into smaller, lower cost and locally responsive businesses. Following Midland Red in 1981, Western National was set to be split into four bus-operating companies from January 1983, with secretarial services continuing to be provided for all four companies at Exeter and engineering support from the Laira Bridge works in Plymouth. Shortly after I returned from that course, several colleagues sadly found they would lose their jobs.

In Cornwall and West Devon, the Western National identity was retained under a new company known simply as Western National without the 'Omnibus Company' appendage. In south Devon, where the Devon General fleetname had survived on green buses, a new Devon General was formed with buses painted red once more. North Devon Red Bus covered the

area indicated by its title, with a darker red livery.

The Southern National name was revived in Somerset and Dorset, causing some residents to question when was it ever anything else. The original Southern National covered Weymouth and Yeovil, but north Somerset services were always Western National. With the 1983 change, a large sign was placed in front of Weymouth's switchboard to remind the operator "We are now Southern National – again!".

For me, now with the new Southern National, responsibility gradually increased to cover the Bridport and Lyme Regis operations.

Since a few buses were transferred between the new companies to make up suitable allocations, I was asked if I still had a requirement for an open-topper. In answering "yes" and "I'll take two if they are available", the opportunity was seized to have two of the ex-Devon General convertible VRTs transferred to Weymouth.

Most of the fleet had vinyl stickers applied to change

fleetnames and legal address for the new company, but from the outset it was suggested the open top buses should have a largely cream livery (having learned the lesson from Weston-super-Mare) and carry new names appropriate for Dorset. This followed accordingly, but adopting a non-corporate livery was still very daring then and was done with some trepidation. In the event, nobody from NBC raised any objections and the open-top VRTs became flagships for the company, joined later by further VRTs which became permanent open-top.

The livery was very popular and the local trade union was so impressed it asked if the whole fleet could be repainted in this style, whereupon it was necessary to explain what corporate livery was and why this would not be permitted.

A further livery variation, with additional areas of white, also appeared for service X35 which ran along the south coast between Portland, Weymouth, Poole and Bournemouth. In the new Western National, Plymouth-area buses

received more white as part of a scheme to emphasise coordination with Plymouth City Transport buses on joint services..

A new coach livery

Coaching activities increased across Southern National with additional National Express work taken on, requiring the acquisition of extra coaches. Local express services were developed with the X96 between Taunton and Bristol launched during September 1983, while a drive to increase private hire reflected efforts to expand the business.

NBC was relaxing its policy towards coach liveries, with striped — sometimes referred to as venetian blind — variations allowed for express services and local coaching. Instead of green and white for local coaches, Southern National introduced brown and yellow house colours on white, with a hint of the Great Western Railway's (GWR) historic livery. This was appropriate in view of the GWR's historic connections with the original National companies in the West Country.

BELOW: **The King's Statue, Weymouth in July 1983 with named open-top VRTs** *Thomas Hardy* **and** *Lawrence of Arabia*, **both of whom had local connections, daringly wearing their new livery of NBC green with prominent areas of Tilling rather than NBC leaf cream.**
MARTIN S CURTIS

ABOVE: Marshall-bodied Bristol LHS 92 (VOD 92K) at Bridport in July 1985. Several of these 33-seaters, new to Devon General, were used in the area, where many rural routes were barely passable even with this size of vehicle.
IAIN MacGREGOR

BELOW: Southern National's new coach colours of brown and yellow stripes on white displayed at Radipole Lake in August 1985 on Plaxton Panorama Elite-bodied Bristol RELHs 2398, 2421 and 2393.
MARTIN S CURTIS

National Express livery remained predominantly white with red and blue, but versions with stripes appeared here too, and as service standards improved in the face of more competition, Rapide services were developed with on-board toilets together with hostesses providing at-seat light refreshments.

Additional new Dennis Falcon V and Leyland Tiger coaches were acquired, and later still a pair of double-deck MCW Metroliners. The first Tigers perpetuated the Western National fleetnumbering system but it was then decided that these and other frontline coaches should be numbered SN1 upwards to emphasise the company's presence in express coach circles.

We occupied a new Southern National head office at St James Street, Taunton during the year, replacing temporary accommodation in the existing Taunton premises. Some functions and secretarial staff remained for a while at Exeter. For some, this meant relocating from Exeter to Taunton while several new managers were also

appointed. Several of Southern National's most senior officials, however, were transferred from the original company, which assisted in providing continuity and an established knowledge of the territory.

Modern ticket machines

Western National had continued to use Setright ticket machines even when services were converted to one-man operation, but was unusual among NBC operators in not adding motorised units to speed up ticket issuing; they had remained hand-operated, requiring the driver to turn a handle on machines attached to the cab door.

Furthermore, machines were allocated to individual drivers rather than requiring them to be shared between staff. This allowed unscrupulous staff the opportunity to interfere with the workings of Setright machines.

At the end of 1983, Timtronic electronic ticket machines, mounted to vehicles and able to record a wealth of background data, were introduced across the south-west, including with

Southern National. Revenue soared at one particular depot. This was not a reflection of the established residents who were employees at this location, since average length of service of the culprits was very low – in complete contrast with the general situation, including those at surrounding depots. It did reflect a situation that occurred sometimes, where staff from other areas (including those already with NBC) visited a holiday location and sought employment there.

There is always a risk of dishonesty wherever cash handling takes place, but what was so unfortunate for an operator in the West Country where populations and revenue tended to be low, was that further cash losses had a serious impact on investment, the affordability of meeting wages and other costs, and even the ability to maintain some services. But while the effect was significant, most employees were honest and unaware of the activities of a dishonest minority.

The new Southern National achieved a great deal in its first year, but there was still time to look back. To mark the 50th anniversary of the last GWR bus service in Weymouth, two VRTs were fitted with commemorative headboards from December 1983. This was organised in conjunction with British Rail, the Dorset Transport Circle and Southern National inspector Brian Jackson, who was a prolific transport writer and historian. The GWR service ran between Radipole, the town centre and

should all be identical so any key would be suitable for any bus. Southern National failed to do this, and when an inspector dropped a box of keys shortly after their introduction, it took a considerable time to find which fitted a particular vehicle. Very rapidly thereafter, all keys were numbered to identify which minibus it fitted.

The Transport Act 1985 had by now been enacted and not only would deregulation of services follow from October 1986, but the privatisation of NBC subsidiaries would also proceed. The first operating company sold was Devon General, to its management in August 1986. Western National was sold a year later while Southern National and North Devon (Red Bus), sold together to management, were almost the last to go, in March 1988.

Southern National experimented with different fleetname styles and colour schemes, including minibus colours and a blue scheme on VRTs, but most big buses to be repainted (which was a slow process) carried a Southdown-inspired light green and cream.

By then, I had accepted a post elsewhere, but have retained a keen interest in the former Western National area. Sadly, many bus stations and depots have closed since then, and while NBC was not perfect, it offered a structured, carefully managed transport system, with long-term opportunities for those seeking a career in transport. •

seafront, but was absorbed into the original Southern National's town services from January 1934.

Minibuses arrive

A bus service revolution began during 1984 when, as an experiment, Devon General introduced the first of a large fleet of Ford Transit minibuses in Exeter, in place of conventional vehicles. In anticipation of future competition, these robust, 16-seaters ran at high frequencies, encouraging minimal waiting times for passengers and flooding the streets, which would make it extremely difficult for another operator to compete.

Although cramped with limited luggage space, and necessitating the recruitment of many additional drivers, they generated increased passenger numbers in the short term and NBC regarded the experiment as a success. Other subsidiaries were encouraged to follow and Southern National introduced similar minibuses on selected services across its networks.

Minibuses protected operators when competition was threatened and NBC fleets across England and Wales began to introduce

them. No longer did corporate liveries apply, and new marketing brands and a wide range of colours appeared on the minibus fleets, most but not all of which were based on Ford Transits.

Southern National's minibuses were branded Shuttle and the first ran in Taunton during autumn 1985, painted deep red and cream. Weymouth's followed in July the following year, painted yellow with orange and blue bands, and more appeared in Yeovil, Bridgwater, Chard and Bridport with each location having its own distinctive colours.

Some operators specified that as each Transit had its own ignition key, their locks

LEFT: Two Roe-bodied Leyland Olympians were purchased ex-West Yorkshire PTE in 1987. While repainted in NBC leaf green and white, 509 (UWW 9X) displays no NBC symbols. A Ford Transit minibus is behind it on route E — all minibus routes were identified by letters rather than numbers.
COLIN L CADDY

MIDDLE: Southern National experimented with several fleetname styles and liveries after it was sold to its managers, including this blue scheme in 1988 on VRT 602 (LWG 845P), one of ten transferred from Yorkshire Traction in 1982.
MARTIN S CURTIS

BELOW: The company settled on this Southdown-style livery, seen in Weymouth in August 1990 on ECW-bodied Leyland Olympian 1814 (A686 KDV), which has the last chassis built by Bristol Commercial Vehicles before Leyland closed its factory in 1983. It was delivered to Devon General in December that year and had recently been acquired by Southern National, which retained its original fleetnumber.
MARTIN S CURTIS

SUBSCRIBE TO BUSES

AND RECEIVE YOUR FREE GIFT WORTH OVER £14!

SAVE UP TO 45%*

Choose your package...

Then get your FREE gift...

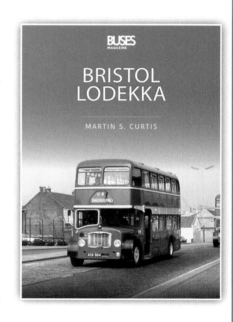

BRISTOL LODEKKA

A re-issue of the much-loved title, *Bristol Lodekka: In colour*. Lodekkas first appeared in service during a period when the passenger-transport industry was enjoying a peak in popularity and passenger numbers were among their highest ever in the provinces.

From the Editor

Buses Magazine, we bring you the latest bus news, whether that be from a business, enthusiast or preservation perspective, along with numerous exclusive features every issue. No other magazine takes such a comprehensive look at the bus industry, past and present.

With our detailed Fleet News section, dedicated global, London, business and preservation pages, monthly letters and book and model reviews, there is no better single source for all things bus related.

Don't miss out on this great subscription offer!

James Day
Editor

When networks were **redrawn**

The National Bus Company ended the 1970s with a plan to find out why people did and did not use its services and tore up and rebuilt many decades old networks to meet the needs of a changing world. ROGER DAVIES explains what MAP was, what it achieved and what it felt like for the people who implemented it.

The bus industry is relatively young. It grew up following World War One as a result of the increased reliability of the internal combustion engine and availability of vehicles and people who could drive and maintain them when no longer required by the military.

Bus and truck businesses boomed, giving greater accessibility and flexibility than ever before, creating a transport revolution larger than those of railways and canals before it. By the 1930s, buses were the dominant mode of public transport, with railways closing lines and stations no longer fit for purpose.

In this environment there was little need for market research, but World War Two had a different effect, and arguably it was the start of significant car use. Coupled with other changes in lifestyle, bus usage began to decline from the early 1950s onwards, so the need to understand the way things were going became more significant. But an industry built on expansion was ill equipped to deal with decline and its once-strong finances began to deteriorate. It was slow to change.

A pioneering attempt at market research was made during the 1960s by Geoff Harding, general manager of Wallasey Corporation's bus service, using prepaid postcards to find out travel needs. But largely the industry reaction was to cut mileage and frequencies, which often left buses and crews in depots when they could have been earning something.

With the bus industry generally losing passengers, the industry became increasingly reliant on outside funding. The Transport Act 1968 gave local authorities powers to fund loss-making services. Some did, but the 1970s began with service withdrawals and depot closures in several areas, just as the state-owned National Bus Company (NBC) was established. New bus grant from central government met part of the capital cost of replacing fleets.

From 1974, local authorities in England and Wales assumed a coordinating role over bus services and had a greater incentive to fund loss makers. Companies such as Western National, with huge swathes of rural territory, were especially under pressure. Difficult decisions needed to be taken, but unfortunately many networks, under network or agency agreements, simply continued as before with no investigation into whether routes — or sections of them — were still appropriate. With rapidly rising costs, this led to well used services being cut to provide resources for little used ones, a completely unsustainable situation. Something had to be done.

VNP becomes MAP

As it tried to adjust to a new life following the sale of its most profitable operations to West Midlands PTE in 1973, NBC's Midland Red subsidiary devised a computer-based system in 1977 designed to clearly identify what was financially strong and what was weak. It was very accurately called the Viable Network Project (VNP), but this name was felt to be too blunt to sell to local councils, so it was renamed Market Analysis Project (MAP).

The idea remained as first conceived, to clearly demonstrate in a structured way where losses were being made so councils had a firm base to justify their spending. Odd though it may seem today was the key fact that it was computer based, as previously timetables had been produced by bus companies either typed or handwritten. Now they were computer generated and the impact was impressive.

It worked. By and large councils loved it and even stumped up large sums of money to fund the expensive surveys.

It was viewed a bit differently within NBC. The company centrally had a rather odd approach to its management out in the field. While on the one hand trusting them with huge staffs and assets, in other cases it seemed to believe things would only get done if firm and indisputable instruction was given. Granted it was dealing with a widely varying bunch of managers, but nevertheless this attitude was less than widely appreciated.

Given the perceived importance of MAP, the instructions to do it were even more strong and no dispute was tolerated. Regional MAP coordinators were appointed to explain and enforce the project often to sceptical audiences.

To make matters worse, NBC decided the process would be carried out in secret. The supervising teams, chosen from existing staff, were locked away in offices and buses, with operating staff forbidden to visit them lest their views pollute the purity of the data. It was not a recipe for harmony and was completely unenforceable and also meant that MAP was viewed with some distaste by those who would ultimately have to introduce and run the results. It was all unnecessary, as nobody doubted the need for action and everyone realised the existing situation could not continue.

So what went on in those secret offices and buses? Geoff Price, who worked as a supervisor on MAP at Ribble in north-west England gives an insight.

All bus stops there had to be identified and numbered physically, either by bus or car. These identifications were put on lists for the on-board surveyors. Every person on every trip on every route was interviewed and asked where they we going from and to, and the purpose of their trip. School holidays and bank holidays were avoided.

Surveyors were recruited from local job centres as required. Supervisors were on duty throughout the operating day, planning surveyors' duties, arranging transport for them and ensuring any journeys missed were covered.

Results from the on-board surveys were processed as soon as they were received. This was a huge task and some surveying staff were kept on to help. The results went through the MAP computer system in Birmingham and the resets used to draw conclusions of what changes were necessary, if any, to existing services.

At the end of the process, the finished scheme was presented as a fait accompli, very much a case of "computer says yes".

Midland Red set the pace
Ahead of the game was, naturally, Midland Red. It was seen to set the way these things were done. As each scheme was introduced it was accompanied by a local branding applied to the relevant buses and carried through including drivers' ties. For the bus tie collector these were glory days.

The Midland Red brand names were Avonbus (Stratford), Chaserider (Cannock and Stafford, recently revived by new owner Centrebus as the name of its local company), Hotspur (Shrewsbury and Ludlow), Hunter (Nuneaton), Lancer (Coalville and Swadlincote), Leamington & Warwick, Mercian (Tamworth), Reddibus (Redditch), Ridercross (Banbury), Rugby, Severnlink (Worcester, Malvern, Bromsgrove), Stratford Blue (in place of Avonbus), Tellus (Telford), Wandaward (Hereford and Ledbury), Wayfarer (Evesham) and Wendaway (Kidderminster).

With a few exceptions like Stratford Blue, NBC could not swallow local identities, so the buses remained stubbornly NBC Midland Red with the local branding stuck on, neither one thing nor the other, Along with some of the brands being perhaps a bit daft, it must have bemused

ABOVE: Hotspur and NBC branding on Midland Red North 1702 (A702 HVT), a Duple Dominant-bodied Leyland Tiger, in Newcastle-under-Lyme in July 1985. IAIN MacGREGOR

BELOW: London Country's Watfordwide brand on a Leyland National otherwise in standard NBC green. TERRY BLACKMAN

and confused customers. Some
others followed Midland Red's
lead, but others were more
sceptical.

The brand names adopted at
Hants & Dorset, for example,
were a mix of geographical,
historic bus company and
invented. The geographical
ones were South Wessex (Poole,
Bournemouth and Lymington)
and South Hants (Southampton),
the historic company names
were Venture (Basingstoke) and
New Provincial or Provincial
Joint Services (Hants & Dorset
Fareham and Gosport & Fareham
operations), while the invented
ones were Wiltsway (Salisbury
and surrounding areas) and
Winton Line (Winchester).

Alder Valley revived Aldershot
& District as one of its local
subsidiary brands and also used
Kennet Bus in Newbury, while
London Country had Thames-
line and Watfordwide. Some
names were shared between
adjoining NBC companies whose
routes were subject of the same
MAP scheme; examples of these
included Alder Valley and London
Country both using Chilternlink
and Weyfarer, the latter taking
its name from the River Wey and
covering the Guildford area,
the name spelt differently from
Midland Red's Evesham network.

Western National branded its
revised network south of the
River Tamar as Cornish Fairways
in May 1980 but changed it later
to Cornwall Busways. There

were Welsh route brands like
South Wales Transport's Afanway
and Cleddau, National Welsh's
Barrivale, Cynon Dare and Glan-
Ogwr and Crosville's Bws Llyn.

A common feature of many
of the revised networks was to
require fewer vehicles but more
double-deckers on corridors
that demanded greater vehicle
capacity. Midland Red had its
central works cut down some
of its 10m Fords into shorter
midibuses.

MAP at Maidstone & District

As for the outcome, here I
can only speak from my own
experience at Maidstone &
District (M&D). My feeling is that,
largely, MAP achieved its aims
but not without some bumpy bits.
And I experienced those.

One of the positive outcomes
was in Hastings. M&D was a well-
respected name in its area with
the exception of Hastings. Here
the local feeling was that buses
had the county town of a different
county on the side and it did not
go down well. M&D had been
wrong to get rid of the Hastings
name when it absorbed Hastings
Tramways in 1955.

MAP corrected this,
reintroducing the Hastings
name on buses running out of
that town and Rye. It was applied
in NBC style but with colours
running through it making
it very attractive, Three years
later under NBC reorganisation,
Hastings & District became a

separate company, good for both
it and M&D and with its basis in
MAP.

Other schemes were not so
positive, When the Sheerness
scheme was shown to me, I
immediately proclaimed it
hopeless, saying we may as well
pack it in as run that. Offering 2hr
frequencies on what were town
services was frankly preposterous.
The data took no account of local
circumstances and the context in
which the buses ran.

I devised my own scheme and
in a heading them off at the pass
move, got the county council on
my side. Commonsense prevailed
and this was the scheme that
was introduced, subsequently
registered for deregulation, and
continued until fairly recently
when Arriva, M&D's successor,
chucked in the towel.

Another challenge was
Maidstone, This was complicated
by including the long mooted
coordination between M&D and
Maidstone Borough. Indeed, MAP

can be credited with making this happen. It was in both operators' interest as good savings were to be made including the closure of the M&D depot in the town very much in line with NBC national policy on medium-sized towns.

The whole process was complicated by the borough council's desire for its buses to be seen throughout the enlarged council area. The arrangement was based on both operators having the same share of the new network as the old. M&D was the larger contributor by around 61% to 39% which, given the borough's expansionist aims, meant M&D going into areas it had not served before.

To make matters worse, in some circumstances it meant only operating them one day a week. With the local depot closed, all these operations were done by crews from outlying depots. The result, while achieving the aims set for it, was an operational train wreck waiting to happen with

much customer inconvenience. It all took time to sort out, including the establishment of an M&D outstation in the borough's depot.

A visible outcome was the appearance of the Maidstone Area Bus services (MABS) black and yellow logo with the M shaped like Kent oast houses on publicity, borough buses and M&D buses most likely to work MABS services.

With a bit of operational input into the process, the potential disruption to passengers in Sheerness and actual in Maidstone would have been avoided.

Exported to Scotland

NBC also "exported" MAP to the Scottish Bus Group (SBG) as Scotmap, which Gavin Booth describes in a bit more detail in the chapter starting on p86. The principles and results had many parallels with what happened in England and Wales, including the increased requirement for double-deckers. Many of SBG's

all-stops routes were long ones, connecting cities, towns and intermediate villages, but patronised mainly by passengers making local journeys. Scotmap revisions split many of these up into shorter routes.

MAP was important in breaking the deadlock that was driving the bus industry into an increasing spiral of decline and increasing dependence on public subsidy. It was very similar to deregulation, giving the clear differentiation between sustainable bus services and loss-making ones. Deregulation built on this, adding that local councils had to put out loss-making services to competitive tender rather than negotiate with the established operator. It finally brought cross-subsidy out of the closet, something that remains relevant today.

It is interesting to ponder whether the architects of the Transport Act 1985 used MAP as the basis for some of their proposals. •

BELOW: Maidstone Area Bus Services branding was applied to the vehicles of both M&D and Maidstone Borough Council, operator in December 1983 of Wright-bodied Bedford YMT 140 (CKM 140Y).
TERRY BLACKMAN

A cause for dismay?

Shocked by his first sighting of a double-decker in NBC's poppy red, PETER ROWLANDS was never a fan of the corporate identity — or the thinking behind it on local buses — and was delighted when it was relaxed and eventually abandoned in the mid-1980s

RIGHT: Two preserved 'Queen Mary' Leyland Titan PD3s from the Southdown fleet offer a vivid example of how NBC's corporate livery changed the appearance of vehicles. The one on the left is in corporate leaf green with double-N logo in the same white as the fleetname, the green applied over moulding strips that previously separated the colours. The open-top bus on the right is in the traditional apple green and cream, which on a covered top bus had a cream roof and top deck window surrounds.
ADRIAN ROBERTS

There are many words I could use to describe my reaction on first seeing a double-decker bus in full National Bus Company (NBC) livery in 1972, but perhaps the one that best sums it up is dismay.

I think it was a Leyland Atlantean in the Northern General fleet, so it would previously have been finished in Northern's dark red and cream with a gold fleetname. Now it had been painted in what seemed to me a garish overall red, with a white fleetname that struck me as totally devoid of finesse.

What kind of confused thinking, I wondered, had led the people behind this sudden brash assertion of corporate identity to believe they could take any pride in abandoning an elegant and long-standing local livery and replacing it with such a bland, undistinguished substitute?

I realise many industry lovers have a real fondness for the NBC corporate bus livery. All I can say is that as a bystander who had known life before NBC, I could feel only shock and disappointment when confronted with such a fundamental change in appearance. To me the new livery's artless simplicity looked simply utilitarian. It evoked the allover red livery applied to British Road Services lorries after Britain's road haulage industry was nationalised in 1948. How could such a thing possibly help entice new customers to travel by bus?

There was another dimension, too. Northern General had several subsidiaries with their own individual liveries – Tynemouth & District, for instance, with its cherry red and cream, and Gateshead & District with its green and cream. Now these companies were apparently destined to adopt that same simplistic allover red. Visually, their separate existence was to be more or less obliterated, save for their individual fleetnames – and eventually these too were destined to disappear.

Perhaps worse still, United Automobile Services, an entirely separate company (but also part of NBC), followed suit and adopted the same new poppy red as the Northern General group. Almost at a stroke, visual interest and differentiation among NBC fleets across Tyne & Wear seemed about to disappear. It soon dawned on me that a similar story was being played out in NBC bus fleets right across England and Wales.

Disingenuous slogan
To compound the affront, numerous buses in NBC fleets started to display a disingenuous slogan on the side reading "Proud to be part of the National Bus Company. Together we can really go places". Who, I wondered, could possibly think that making all these fleets look alike would equip them any better for the metaphorical (or real) local journeys they were already making? How was it helpful to make it harder for passengers to pick out the bus they wanted in streets often crowded with others that would now look more or less the same?

Lest I seem to be painting too rosy a picture of what went before, I cannot deny that the former liveries of these various companies sometimes had a common heritage. While the BET group, the former parent of Northern General, never had a single nationwide livery, some of its fleets did tend to have a corporate look – a single solid main colour, sometimes with cream relief applied in varying proportions.

When it came to former Tilling companies, latterly part of the

Transport Holding Company (THC), many of them already had a standard livery in either red or green. Red United buses in Newcastle, for instance, looked more or less identical to red Eastern Counties buses in Norwich, 250miles away.

Yet these liveries were rich in history and meticulous in application, often with fine detailing such as coach lining and gold lettering; and the colours themselves were strong. They were intrinsically elegant. NBC's poppy red, and perhaps to a lesser extent its leaf green, seemed like mocking apologies for the rich Tilling red and green they had supplanted.

There were exceptions to all this. In the Tyne & Wear operating area, for instance, Northern General started turning out some of its subsidiaries' buses

in a yellow and cream version of its new livery to convey a spirit of coordination with the passenger transport executive's (PTE) yellow and cream bus fleet (ironically soon to be yellow and white). Yet arguably these buses looked like exactly what they were: NBC buses in different colours.

Moreover, that yellow seldom looked the same as PTE yellow, even though some historians insist that it was. Others state that it was a specific NBC yellow, not the PTE's cadmium yellow. Whatever the reality, subjectively it seldom looked the same; the underlying colours and the weathering characteristics of the paint no doubt played a part here.

Eventually both Northern and United adopted the full PTE yellow and white livery, and a similar path was followed for NBC

ABOVE: A small variation in the poppy red and white livery of Ribble 1380 (NRN 380P), a Park Royal-bodied Leyland Atlantean, added the Merseyside PTE logo to balance NBC's on routes in the Liverpool city region.
PETER ROWLANDS

BELOW: The yellow version of NBC livery on Northern General 3487 (DVK 487W), an MCW Metrobus. The fleetnames were also in a non-standard colour.
PETER ROWLANDS

buses in the West Yorkshire PTE area.

For a while NBC also allowed a fourth, blue variant of its standard livery for fleets that had previous been predominantly blue – Sunderland District, for instance, and East Yorkshire. Then for no obvious reason it recanted, and required them to be either red or green, illogically leaving one tiny South Wales fleet,

Jones of Aberbeeg, free to soldier on in a non-standard blue.

Fundamental miscalculation
On reflection, it has always struck me that NBC chairman Freddie Wood, who had been recruited in 1971 from outside the bus industry, made a fundamental miscalculation over the new look, applying the same philosophy to local buses

as to express coaches. Whatever one thinks of the white National Express livery he introduced, almost overnight it revealed a national route network that had been hidden behind the disparate liveries of the NBC companies that provided it. It was a clever move that arguably achieved its objective with remarkable success – albeit at the sacrifice of so much tradition.

When Wood applied the same philosophy to buses, there was little if any logic to it. In effect, the organisation was trumpeting a national identity to people who were mostly travelling within a fairly narrow local area, and would have had little or no interest in or awareness of the appearance of buses in other places. Moreover, he was riding roughshod over a pride in local identity that had been cultivated over many decades within the bus companies in question.

But the NBC corporate identity was here to stay, and as the 1970s unfolded it became a fact of life in the bus industry across

England and Wales. NBC buses now all looked more or less the same wherever you went. It was as if a light had gone out. Varying chassis makes and body styles maintained distinctions within and between fleets, but these may well have been lost on a large proportion of the travelling public. The main point of interest now was whether or not single-deckers (and sometimes double-deckers) had the optional white band.

In fairness, when the livery was well maintained I came to realise it could look crisp and bright – although no one could ever accuse it of delivering any kind of elegance or finesse. One change I certainly welcomed was the adoption in 1976 of the full-colour version of the NBC logo to replace the original outline version.

Yet like many industry watchers, I still yearned for the differentiation of the old days – celebrated whenever a vehicle was singled out for painting in a heritage livery. It was hard to believe that much-missed liveries

such as Southdown's apple green and cream could have disappeared forever. So when the 1980s ushered in a new era with talk of deregulation and even privatisation, many hoped to see a relaxation in the NBC's corporate grip on liveries. And magically, it actually started to happen.

Declaration of intent

Gradually, individual companies within the organisation started

to vary their liveries. One of the earliest to make a move was Midland Red East, created in 1981 when Midland Red was broken up into four smaller companies. By the following year it had adopted a new allover red livery – bland in itself, since it lacked even NBC's white relief, but striking because it was a different red. It was an unmistakable declaration of intent.

In 1984 that intent was realised when the company renamed itself Midland Fox, and introduced another new livery, this time with a yellow front end and a diagonal stripe where yellow and red (a new red) abutted on the sides. It now looked like an independent company, although in reality it remained part of NBC until it was privatised three years later.

By 1983 several more NBC subsidiaries were flexing their muscles by adopting new non-standard liveries. South Midland, separated from City of Oxford Motor Services, introduced a maroon and white livery. Hastings & District, similarly separated from Maidstone & District, coincidentally also adopted maroon and white.

Cheltenham & Gloucester, created in 1983 through a split in the giant Bristol Omnibus Company, wanted to underline its separate existence within NBC, so it replaced Bristol's leaf green with two new colours. For Cheltenham, disappointingly, it simply switched back to NBC poppy red, but in Gloucester a

ABOVE: Cambus, created out of the western part of Eastern Counties in 1984, adopted a pale blue and cream interpretation of corporate livery. When sold to its managers, a darker blue was added to the mix. Leyland National 210 (MEX 773P), photographed in Cambridge, came from Eastern Counties.
PETER ROWLANDS

ABOVE: When Badgerline took over the country operations of Bristol Omnibus Company based at Weston-super-Mare, Bristol, Bath and Wells, it adopted this radical application of yellow and green complete with badger logos. ECW-bodied Bristol RELL 1318 (LHT 172L) was operated from Wells.
PETER ROWLANDS

new deep blue and white colour scheme was introduced. The proportions were still pure NBC, but the effect was dramatically different.

Gradually the trickle of new liveries turned into a flood. By 1986, before any of the NBC companies had actually been sold, new or revived colour schemes had been introduced by many more of them, including Badgerline, Bristol Omnibus, Cambus, Hampshire Bus, Northumbria Motor Services, Northern General, Potteries and Southdown. Several of these companies, like those that had already changed their image, were new creations set up to even out the size of the constituent units prior to sale.

Where the change stopped short of an entirely new livery, some companies started applying area branding to the existing colour scheme – for instance, the Tellus identity for Midland Red buses in the Telford area.

Southdown was a landmark

The revival of Southdown's traditional apple green seemed a landmark, though it was applied in a relatively unadventurous layout. Much more radical were the new liveries launched by Badgerline and Bristol City Line after the Bristol company was divided in 1985.

Badgerline opted for vivid yellow and green, while Bristol adopted a striking confection of yellow, red and blue. Both designs included diagonal elements, which would become a common theme in many deregulation-era liveries; and both were a world away from the NBC's uniform red and green.

Arguably the most dramatic new liveries of this period were those introduced by Northumbria Motor Services and North Western, which again were new or re-established companies. They took the vogue for diagonal elements to a new place, applying them in a bold and confident

fashion that paid little or no heed to the form of the underlying vehicle body. Consultancy Hyphen Hayden was responsible for both.

North Western modified its livery later to a more conventional linear style that was easier to maintain, but Northumbria stuck to its new livery for over ten years, only losing it when Arriva's corporate style eventually replaced it.

For a while it seemed that the hopes and expectations of those who had always been uneasy with NBC's corporate look had been realised. Operators who had been hidden by the common NBC identity suddenly became visible on the street again as separate entities, usually linked closely with the area they served. It seemed like a return to bus operation the way it had worked before.

Be careful what you wish for

Be careful what you wish for. It was easy to forget that former bus industry giants such as BET and Tilling had achieved their great size through gradual acquisition of independent companies.

RIGHT: The Bristol City rebranding brought this combination of primary colours in place of leaf green, as applied to Roe-bodied Leyland Olympian 9515 (JHU 914X).
PETER ROWLANDS

LEFT: In the short period before Stagecoach bought the company in 1989, Southdown revived its traditional livery, as on Leyland National 163 (SFJ 139R) in Brighton in April 1987, six months before NBC sold it to its managers. A stylised S logo took the place of the NBC double-N.
PETER ROWLANDS

BELOW LEFT: Hyphen Hayden's bold new livery for Northumbria, formed in September 1986 out of the northern part of United Automobile, on ECW-bodied Bristol VRT 521 (UGR 705R), in Newcastle in April 1987.
PETER ROWLANDS

BELOW RIGHT: The new North Western company, created in September 1986 to take over Ribble's Merseyside services, came with another Hyphen Hayden diagonal design. ECW-bodied Leyland Atlantean 502 (FBV 487W) was new to Ribble in 1980.
PETER ROWLANDS

Privatisation in the mid-1980s was followed by exactly the same process: steady consolidation across the industry. By 2000, the vast majority of privatised NBC companies, along with many former municipal and PTE bus operations, belonged to just five giant groups.

Moreover, three of these – Stagecoach, First and Arriva – adopted uniform liveries for their fleets throughout the land. Arguably these liveries had much more finesse than NBC's plain red and green, but the fact is that they wound back the clock to pre-privatisation times, denying the expression of local identity that had flowered briefly in the 1980s.

What goes around comes around. By the early 2020s First had reintroduced local identities for most of its UK companies, although Arriva and Stagecoach remained equivocal, preferring to brand selected individual services (if anything) rather than the subsidiary companies providing them.

Arguably the corporate heads of the bus industry continue to struggle to understand what those out in the field know by instinct – that local buses need to seem local, regardless of who actually runs them: not necessarily so local that every route has its own identity, but at least local enough to show that the operator relates to the market it is serving.

This was the wisdom NBC so conspicuously failed to grasp when it imposed its corporate identity on its bus fleet – a mistake that perhaps helps explain why all these years later, it can still spark such strong feelings among those who remember it. •

The cross-border
Bristol exchange

The Scottish Bus Group was so disenchanted with the early Bristol VRTs that it bought between 1968 and 1970 that it arranged the exchange of most of them with the National Bus Company for slightly older front-engined Lodekka FLFs. ALAN MILLAR relates what happened and suggests why.

ABOVE: The swap was underway at Western SMT in March 1973 when newly arrived Bristol Lodekka FLF6G B2408 (THN 262F) and soon-to-depart Bristol VRTSL6G B2268 (OCS 594H) were sitting alongside each other in Anderston bus station in Glasgow. The Lodekka had come from United Automobile while the VRT was destined to go to Alder Valley.
IAIN MacGREGOR

Although they both fell under the control of the British Transport Commission (BTC) and Transport Holding Company (THC) for almost 20 years, the Scottish Bus Group (SBG) and its Tilling group counterparts in England and Wales had little day-to-day involvement in one another's affairs.

Cross-border services operated jointly by Eastern Scottish and United Automobile predated state ownership. Likewise those provided by Western SMT and Ribble, which became state-owned in 1968 when BET sold its British bus businesses.

Those two SBG companies operated their mainly overnight coach services linking Edinburgh and Glasgow with London without any input from state-owned operators at the London end, other than for London Transport — a companion organisation within BTC — providing garaging, cleaning and fuelling services. SBG had its own ticket sales office in London, in Regent Street near Oxford Circus in premises that today house a Pret A Manger takeaway shop.

Tilling, SBG and BET each developed their own managers, as did SBG and the National Bus Company (NBC) when it was formed; careers were progressed either within Scotland or within England and Wales.

The same can be said of vehicles. There were no routine cross-border exchanges of rolling stock. The nearest, and certainly the biggest event along those lines came between 1951 and 1953 when SBG took advantage of its status within BTC to buy 129 of the 435 wartime utility Guy Arabs surplus to London Transport's requirements and put 118 of them into service.

That was an astute purchase, not the dumping of London cast-offs on unfortunate Scots. The Scottish Motor Traction (SMT) group was a regular purchaser of secondhand vehicles as well as new ones and SBG replaced the bodies on 37 of the Guys; ten became longer single-deckers and ten were disguised as 'tin front' Arab IVs.

All of which underlines that there was no precedent for the deals that bound the state-owned groups together between 1971

and 1974 when SBG exchanged 106 of its 109 Bristol VRTs for the same number of slightly older Bristol Lodekka FLFs in seven NBC fleets.

No prior history

SBG had no prior history of buying Bristols when it became state-owned. Central SMT was allocated an 'unfrozen' K5G double-decker in 1942 and Western SMT inherited 18 Bristols (Ks and single-deck Ls) when it absorbed the Caledonian Omnibus Company in 1950.

Leyland, AEC, Guy, Daimler and Bedford were its favoured suppliers when it was SMT, but with BTC determined to make good Bristol's loss of third party business and meet a proportion of its new vehicle requirement, that was set to change, and between 1954 and 1968, when it was under BTC and THC control, SBG ordered 1,478 Bristols while continuing to buy from some of its previously favoured manufacturers.

There may have been an obligation to buy chassis from Bristol and bodies from ECW, but the Scottish group was highly selective in what it purchased. It only wanted them with six-cylinder Gardner engines, so no Gardner 5LWs or Bristol's own AVW or BVW. Bristol lent it examples of the SC (a rural single-decker of similar configuration to the Bedford SB) and the later SUL (a state-built equivalent of the Albion Nimbus) but it was insufficiently impressed to buy any. Nor did it buy any of the ECW-bodied MW single-

decker that was a staple in many Tilling fleets. All of the Bristols it ordered before 1967 had manual rather than semi-automatic gearboxes.

ECW built the bodies on 1,317 of the Bristols, the coachwork finished to a generally higher specification – particularly of seat upholstery – than was the norm in England and Wales.

The selective purchasing extended farther than the models it did not buy. Scottish Omnibuses, which traded as Eastern Scottish from 1964, bought 50 ECW-bodied LS6G and 20 MW6G touring coaches between 1954 and 1958, Alexander's bought 20 ECW-bodied LS6G buses in 1955, while Western SMT exercised its independence in such matters by taking 19 LS6Gs in 1957 and 52 MW6Gs between 1958 and 1962 with semi-coach Alexander bodies – the only examples of

either chassis bodied by anyone other than ECW.

Orders placed in the last years of THC ownership included 90 RE coaches with Alexander bodies, mainly for the London services, and 12 RELL6Gs with ECW bus bodies for the Alexander (Fife) fleet.

SBG exercised its obligation to buy Bristol and ECW products mainly by taking the Lodekka, of which 1,106 were delivered between 1955 and 1967. As the first lowheight double-decker to go into production with centre gangways on both decks, this model was ahead of the pack when it became available from 1953, although SBG continued to buy Leyland Titan PD2s and PD3s with lowbridge side sunken gangway bodies until 1961, and some of its Lodekkas replaced highbridge double-deckers on urban routes.

Lodekkas were in six of its seven fleets by 1963 and accounted for all but 24 of the 260 double-deckers supplied to Scottish Omnibuses/Eastern Scottish between 1956 and 1966.

SBG bought more of the original LD model (578) than the flat-floor F-series (528) and bought 154 of its LDs in 1960/61 after the Tilling companies switched to the F-series. Western SMT bought two of the 30ft rear-entrance FL model, the least common of all Lodekkas with just 43 others built for four Tilling fleets. Central SMT bought 48 of

LEFT: Among the ECW-bodied Bristols that SBG companies tried out but did not buy was the front-engined SC rural single-decker. Eastern National 396 (725 APU), the second prototype built in 1954, was loaned to Alexander's southern area the following year. It was an SCX6P with six-cylinder Perkins engine; most production vehicles had the four-cylinder Gardner 4LK.
JIM THOMSON

BELOW: The Scottish companies' love affair with the Lodekka began early in 1955 when Western SMT GB1155 (GCS 241), from its initial delivery of 20 LD6Gs, was newly into service in the Greenock area. It had the original 'long apron' grille that was a feature of early production Lodekkas.
JIM THOMSON

the 27ft forward-entrance FSF between 1961 and 1963, more than any of the Tilling fleets.

SBG bought 101 of the LD's direct successor, the 27ft rear-entrance FS, between 1961 and 1964. It took 376 forward-entrance FLFs, of which 250 were the original 30ft version with up to 70 seats and 126 the 31ft model with extended rear overhang and up to 78 seats; outside Scotland, only Eastern National bought the longer version and its had no more than 70 seats.

Birth of the VR

Bristol had no reason to believe that this could not continue when it introduced its new rear-engined double-deck chassis, conceived as the N type but changed to

the VR when the first two VRX prototypes, 33ft (10m) long with an in-line engine in the offside corner and 80-seat ECW bodies, were completed in 1966. One was registered in Bristol for trials in Tilling fleets, while the other was registered in Motherwell and built to full Central SMT specification with fleetnumber BN331, the next in the sequence of B, BE and BL numbers allocated to its Lodekkas.

It went on extended loan to Central from January 1967, three months before that company began to take delivery of its final order for 25 Lodekkas.

SBG was attracted by the recent increase in permitted vehicle length and Western SMT bought seven 33ft Daimler

Fleetlines with 83-seat bodies (six by Northern Counties, one Alexander) in 1967, but the industry as a whole — especially the Tilling fleets in England and Wales which limited double-deck capacity to 70 seats — wanted a shorter vehicle. That meant a transverse engine and before the year was out Bristol made it known that such a vehicle, the VRT, was in hasty development. The original model became the VRL, but no more were built as British service buses.

SBG placed an order for 25 VRTs for delivery to Eastern Scottish in 1968, its first rear-engined double-deckers other than two Fleetlines that were a byproduct of its acquisition of Baxter's of Airdrie in 1962. Like the seven Western Fleetlines, these were 33ft long 83-seaters. They were the first VRTs to be built and went into service on routes around Glasgow and Edinburgh in November and December 1968.

They also were the only 33ft VRTs that ECW bodied in the 13 years that the model was produced. The New Bus Grant scheme introduced in 1968 subsidised 25% (later 50%) of the price of new buses, but had strict rules on what it did and did not cover, especially in the earliest years. Grant was available for highbridge 33ft double-deckers, but not for their lowheight counterpart; it would appear that

SBG's interest in such vehicles failed to be noticed by or made known to the civil servants who framed the rules.

Consequently, there were no more 33ft Fleetlines for SBG and when it placed its orders in 1968 for a further 94 VRTs, these were on the shorter 30ft 5in chassis. There were to be ten for Eastern Scottish, 20 for Central SMT and 39 for Western SMT, all with ECW bodies with either 75 or 77 seats. Alexander (Midland) also ordered 15, but these were to be bodied by Alexander, a signal of what SBG had in mind for some of its future purchases.

However, there were major teething troubles from the start. One of the original Eastern Scottish batch shed a wheel which fatally injured a passing pedestrian, although that may not have been a design fault of the chassis. There was insufficient ventilation to cool the engine compartment and gearboxes also caused trouble, all of which required major rectification by Bristol, with most of the 1969 delivery going straight back there from ECW's Lowestoft works before they were deemed acceptable for Scotland; most went into service in the last quarter of the year. The Midland chassis had still to be bodied.

One of Western's 39 caught fire while operating a local service in Paisley in 1970 and received a new ECW body the following year.

Missing from order programme

The delayed 1969 vehicles were just entering service when SBG announced its order programme for 1970, its first since being taken out of THC control and no longer tied so closely to Bristol and ECW.

The group was making it known to the trade press that the VRTs were "plagued" (its word) with teething problems, which helps explain why the model would never figure again in its capital investment programmes, which for the next eight years were overseen by Roddie MacKenzie, the executive director responsible for engineering and until 1969 the general manager of Eastern Scottish where most of the VRT problems had manifested themselves.

MacKenzie was one of few SBG senior managers of his generation to have graduated from university and he had

ABOVE: Eastern Scottish AA283 (LFS 283F), fourth of the 25 VRTLL6G 83-seaters whose teething troubles seemed to seal the fate of all of SBG's VRTs. It was operating a busy local service in Glasgow and by March 1972 its bodywork was showing signs of neglect. ALAN MILLAR

LEFT: Central SMT BN357 (NGM 157G), the first of 20 VRTSL6Gs delivered in 1969 after undergoing pre-delivery rectification work, in Dumbarton in March 1970. It went to Eastern Counties in the big exchange. IAIN MacGREGOR

wider industry experience than his peers, having earlier in his career been general manager of the Warrington and Halifax municipal undertakings, appointments separated by three years in road haulage as a regional chief engineer with the BTC's British Road Services. He had clear expectations of what a bus had to deliver for a commercially-focused operator like SBG and the Lodekka had left a good impression in his 13 years at Eastern Scottish.

The 1970 order called for 120 Fleetlines, of which 93 would be the group's first with ECW bodies. Given the content of the 1969 order and the companies that were to receive them, there is cause to believe that those 93 had been pencilled in as VRTs before the full extent of the teething problems became apparent. There were 35 for Central SMT which had no Fleetlines, 20 for Eastern Scottish which only had two, 14 for Alexander (Fife) which had Fleetlines but bought Lodekkas until 1967, and 12 each for Alexander (Midland) and Western SMT. Alexander and Northern Counties were to body the other 27 Fleetlines for Western.

That plan was changed soon after, as it was decided to have the 15 VRTs for Midland bodied by ECW and for Alexander to body the 12 Fleetlines ordered by Western. If SBG was not to buy

any more VRTs, there was little point in Alexander designing a lowheight body for those 15 (it built highbridge bodies later in the 1970s on VRTs for three municipal fleets) and there was no great need to add ECW to the body mix on Western's Fleetlines. Those 12 Fleetlines ended up being diverted to the Fife fleet.

Bristol introduced its improved Series 2 VRT in 1970, but SBG chose not to buy any. Nor did it buy many more Bristols of any type, just a further 46 RE coaches and 70 lightweight LH buses, all with Alexander bodies; the last arrived in 1972.

Time to say goodbye

The VRX prototype was never taken into SBG ownership and was returned to Bristol in 1970, a clue of what was to come.

Also that year, Eastern Scottish rebuilt an eight-year-old FLF for one-man operation. It may never have been operated without a conductor as the layout was unlikely to have been the most appealing for drivers, but it was lent to NBC's Cumberland Motor Services in 1971 (when it also may or may not have run in service) and was de-converted in 1972 by adding a second bulkhead behind the cab. Nonetheless, here was a clear sign of the Bristol double-decker that SBG still preferred.

A deal was agreed in mid-1971 to sell the 15 Midland VRTs, SBG's newest, to Eastern National in exchange for the same number FLFs new between 1965 and 1967; Eastern National had newer FLFs but these would have introduced the semi-automatic variant into SBG which only knew and preferred to stick with manual gearboxes on Lodekkas. Midland allocated them the next 15 numbers in its MRD class for Lodekkas.

In 1972, Western SMT engaged S&N Motors, a bus and coach dealer in Glasgow, to sell its VRTs to anyone who might want them. China Motor Bus considered them for use in Hong Kong, but bought London Transport's XA-class Leyland Atlanteans instead. Western disposed of three through the dealership — two (one of them the recently rebodied one) to Osbornes of Tollesbury in Essex (which also bought both of the VRX prototypes around the same time) and one to Richardsons, a prominent

property developer in the West Midlands — before SBG instructed its subsidiaries to let it negotiate a single deal with NBC for the remaining 91 vehicles on terms that took account of the greater age of the Lodekkas and the new bus grant paid for the VRTs.

The NBC buses selected for transfer were its newest FLFs with manual gearboxes, from Bristol's 236th sanction built in 1967/68. Forty-three were with Eastern Counties, 12 with Alder Valley, 11 with Northern General and its Tynemouth subsidiary, nine with United Automobile, seven with Southdown-Brighton Hove & District, four with United Counties, three with Southern Vectis and two with Bristol Omnibus Company.

The Northern General and Tynemouth vehicles had only recently moved there from United in exchange for Daimler Fleetlines; neither the Lodekkas nor the Fleetlines — which were required for an expansion of one-man operation — were at all standard in either of the NBC fleets that then had them, so it was determined that the 20 Scottish VRTs sent in exchange would all go to United and the

unfamiliar Fleetlines return to Northern.

For all the meticulous planning that went into the exchange, one important fact was missed. The United Counties and Bristol Omnibus Lodekkas were FLF6Bs with Bristol BVW engines. All the others had Gardner 6LX or (in the case of the Southern Vectis trio) 6LW engines, which suited SBG just fine. These six were destined for Eastern Scottish and the issue only hit home when the first of the United Counties quartet reached Edinburgh, was placed into service before there was time to repaint it (both fleets'

livery was green) and someone lifted the bonnet to be greeted by something he did not recognise.

This was all resolved quickly. United Counties 736 was returned to Northampton and all six FLF6Bs were taken out of the exchange, replaced by the next newest FLF6Gs which also were built in 1967: three more from Eastern Counties, two from Alder Valley and one from Southdown-BH&D.

Eastern Counties provided half of the FLFs sent to the three Scottish fleets — 46 out of 91 — but it only received 30 VRTs in exchange, as ten went instead

ABOVE: Central SMT BE372 (RHN 945F), previously Northern General 2862 and United 945 before that, in Lanark in September 1977 on a trunk service from Glasgow. IAIN MacGREGOR

FLFs into service

The SBG companies took different approaches to putting the English FLFs into service. Central SMT was the most thorough, repainting them all and replacing their destination displays with the group's standard triangular arrangement. It also gave them the same fleetnumbers in its sequence for Bristol double-

to Lincolnshire Road Car and six to Eastern National, which both transferred older FLFs to Eastern Counties. NBC was more likely than SBG to operate the VRTs without conductors, so that helped meet their operational requirements. It also balanced the age of the Eastern Counties fleet.

deckers as the VRTs they replaced, with a BE prefix instead of BN.

Eastern Scottish and Western SMT took longer to change the destination displays and put some vehicles in service without an immediate repaint. Eastern Scottish numbered them neatly at the end of its numerical sequence as AA965 to AA999, while Western gave its 36 FLFs the next numbers in its chronological series, B2406 to B2441, in the random order in which they arrived. Eight of the Eastern Scottish vehicles were painted in the blue and grey livery of its Baxter's fleet in Airdrie.

Southern Vectis gave its three ex-SBG VRTs (one from Central,

two from Eastern Scottish) the same numbers (619 to 621) as the FLFs they replaced.

While Eastern National had placed ex-Midland VRTs in service in their former owner's blue and cream, most of the 91 were repainted in the poppy red or leaf green of their recipient fleet before entering service; most retained their SBG destination displays initially, some turned upside down so the destination was above the three-track route number display. When first received, Eastern Counties painted former Eastern Scottish AA280 (the first VRT built) as an overall advertisement for Courage beer, complete with a slogan — Courage comes to Norwich — that caused some mirth in Scottish circles.

Twelve of the 33ft long 83-seat VRTs went to Eastern Counties, which retained their high seating capacity, but Eastern National reconfigured the three it received to match the 70-seat capacity of its existing FLFs and VRTs (it had already taken seven seats out of the ex-Midland ones and did the same to the one it got from Western). Alder Valley removed five seats from its two 83-seaters, while Southdown reduced most of its eight to 74-seaters, achieved

RIGHT: Eastern Scottish put eight of its ex-NBC Lodekkas into the Baxter's fleet in Airdrie, which already had FLFs but had not run VRTs. AA995 (RHN 948V) came from United Automobile. The Alexander-bodied double-decker on the far left was DD961 (9961 SF), SBG's first Daimler Fleetline. IAIN MacGREGOR

LEFT: Among the ex-SBG VRTs that were rebuilt as open-toppers was United 643 (OCS 583H), ex-Western SMT B2253, operating the sea front service in Scarborough in July 1983.
IAIN MacGREGOR

MIDDLE: Three ex-SBG VRTs with Lincolnshire Road Car. Nearest the camera is 1982 (NGM 169G) ex-Central SMT. To the left, either side of a Lodekka LD6G, are 1986 (NCS 435G) and 1987 (NCS 436G) ex-Western SMT. While the other three SBG companies had their VRTs trimmed with then standard cream window rubbers, Western SMT specified black rubbers on its 39.
MARTIN S CURTIS COLLECTION

partly by removing the five-person bench at the back of the lower saloon.

Both parties appeared happy with the vehicles they got. SBG withdrew the FLFs from service between 1978 and 1983, with Eastern Scottish the last to operate them in quantity. The last of all were some of the oldest of the 106, two of five of the ex-Eastern National buses transferred in 1979 from Midland to Alexander (Northern), until then the only SBG fleet never to have run Lodekkas.

At least 47 of the VRTs were still in NBC service in 1984, including all ten of those sent to Lincolnshire and the three with Southern Vectis on the Isle of Wight. Among these were seven of the original 25, the 33ft VRTs

whose performance had sealed the fate of the type in Scotland, buses that by then were 16 years old. Some were converted to open-top and a few were moved between NBC fleets, with those 47 including 11 of the 15 ex-Midland

vehicles transferred from Eastern National to Crosville in 1982.

Today, with First and Stagecoach having businesses either side of the Scotland/England border, vehicles often are moved around Britain as those groups' needs demand, and Stagecoach transferred several ex-NBC Series 3 Bristol VRTs into Scotland in the 1990s, introducing a model that might have been commonplace in the SBG fleet mix had the introduction of the original vehicles gone better than it did. The exchange of SBG's VRTs for NBC's Lodekka FLFs around 50 years ago was something different. A unique arrangement between two related organisations with radically different ideas about the vehicles they wanted to operate. •

BELOW: SBG's decision to sell its VRTs meant that none ever operated for Alexander (Fife) and that the group never bought the improved Series 2 and Series 3 versions, but this picture imagines what an early Series 3 might have looked like in Fife livery. Fife had 145 Lodekkas delivered new between 1956 and 1967 and ordered 14 more that were diverted to Central SMT before delivery in 1965.
KEITH McGILLIVRAY

Mapping, splitting **and** selling

After decades of profitable stability, SBG entered the 1980s embracing a succession of changes as it surveyed and recast its networks, split large companies into smaller units and then faced the inevitability of being privatised, as GAVIN BOOTH explains

In retrospect, nobody could ever pretend that the Scottish Bus Group (SBG) was a thrusting organisation at the cutting edge of technology. And that, perhaps, was the secret of its success over its 40-year existence. It provided bus services over much of mainland Scotland with little fuss, carried millions of passengers each year and was profitable.

With the help of significant investment by the railway companies after 1929, its

predecessor, the Scottish Motor Traction (SMT) group, had brought together the well-established SMT company and the massive Alexander empire, and created two new companies, Central SMT and Western SMT from businesses it had acquired.

In 1949 the group and its four companies passed into state control under the British Transport Commission (BTC) but there was little outward change, except perhaps for SMT passengers in the east of Scotland, whose buses became

green rather than blue. Members of the families who created three of these companies – the Alexanders, the Dicks at Central and the Swords at Western – continued to run their own businesses in their own way, and as long as they were financially successful, they were allowed to do this.

Rural operations in areas like Perthshire, the Borders and south-west Scotland were cross-subsidised by the money-spinning routes in central Scotland; there were urban services in

important towns and a significant interurban network throughout the country. Outside Scotland's four surviving municipal operations – in Aberdeen, Dundee, Edinburgh and Glasgow – the group flourished with only a few pockets where independent operators were (from its perspective) irritatingly well established in these regulated days.

The group had grown in the 1930s by a combination of natural expansion and steadily buying out independent and small municipal operators, and would continue to do this.

The profitable bus services allowed three of the companies to indulge in long-distance services and tours and, looking back, a disproportionate amount of time, money and effort was spent on these. Alexanders, Scottish Omnibuses (as the SMT company had, perhaps misleadingly, been renamed) and Western SMT all ran long-distance services, some all-year round and others in high summer; Scottish Omnibuses (which branded itself as Eastern Scottish in 1964) and Western ran the high-profile Scotland-London services as well as cross-border services with English-based companies.

Alexanders and Scottish Omnibuses had extensive day and extended tour programmes. Central SMT – the group's cash cow for many years – had little time for such fripperies and concentrated on the business of making a lot of

money from its networks in industrial Lanarkshire and west Dunbartonshire.

Conservative purchasing
The group's vehicle policy was equally conservative. It placed annual orders, but each company was allowed to specify its requirements. As part of BTC and its THC successor, it was required to buy a proportion of its new buses from Bristol and Eastern Coach Works (ECW), an obligation it discharged mainly by purchasing over 1,100 Lodekkas. Otherwise, Leylands were popular, except at Scottish Omnibuses, which was not a Leyland fan and until 1966 preferred AECs. Alexander's bought AECs as well as Leylands.

Bodywork was usually entrusted to the Alexander coachbuilding business, now independent of the group, and the end result was often buses and coaches

that were technically robust with big engines, manual gearboxes and well-built bodies designed to carry the maximum number of passengers. So the trusty Leyland Leopard with Alexander Y-type bodywork became a group staple from the mid-1960s onwards, and in bus form provided 53 seats with theoretically space for 24 standees. Central in particular developed a distaste for rear-engined double-deckers and preferred the Leopard/Y type combination for many years.

This recipe kept the group going for its first 20 years or so, but the world was changing. Car ownership was spreading fast and passenger numbers were falling. The group's short-term solution was an annual fares increase, which was usually granted by the traffic commissioners, but when reliability began to suffer in some areas disgruntled passengers started to object and the group

had to look for ways to economise. One fairly blunt instrument was to cut the fleet size, but by the 1970s more drastic measures had become necessary.

Control of SBG had returned to Scotland under the Scottish Transport Group (STG) in 1969, combining the bus companies and the shipping services of what soon became Caledonian MacBrayne. The four SBG companies had grown to five in 1952 with the creation of Highland Omnibuses, and to seven in 1961 when the massive 1,900-bus Alexander empire was split into three companies – Fife, Midland and Northern— formed out of what had been its Fife, Southern and Northern areas. In 1969 SBG's companies had 4,721 vehicles, covering over 168million miles and carrying over 555million passengers.

But any complacency was shattered with local government reorganisation in Scotland in

1975. Ever since the 1930s under SMT and SBG, the bus companies had been in charge of their own destiny with little outside interference, but that was all set to change.

In 1973, Scotland's only passenger transport executive, the Greater Glasgow PTE, was created and two years later Scotland was divided into eight regions and each had responsibility for coordinating road passenger transport services and the establishment of transport policy and programmes for its own patch. Some of these patches were huge. The largest region, Strathclyde, stretched across over 4,700sq miles of mainland and several islands, and was home to around half of Scotland's population.

Now regional officials and politicians were able to influence what the group was doing. In return for support from the regions, which reimbursed SBG

for revenue shortfalls, the group reluctantly had to work closely with the regions.

Scotmap to the rescue
The 1970s proved to be difficult years in more tangible ways. Between 1969 and 1980, passenger journeys fell by nearly 40%, vehicle miles by 26%, staff numbers by 40% and the fleet by 23%. And there were no indications that the situation would improve unless something drastic was done.

The National Bus Company (NBC) had devised the Market Analysis Project (MAP) to check if bus services were in line with passenger demand. An SBG version, Scotmap, was developed and with the help of seconded NBC staff, working with a new tier of senior managers, passenger demand and bus journey time surveys were conducted throughout Scotland and all the major cost elements were examined to produce redesigned and better promoted

service networks that would theoretically place the group in a stronger position for the uncertain days ahead.

The first uncertainty was the deregulation of express services, which exposed the group to on-road competition for the first time, and prompted several established coach operators to try their hand at express operation. More importantly, it prompted a new-start operation that grew to become the Stagecoach empire. SBG's response in 1983 was to create Scottish Citylink from its existing coach services, as described in the next chapter.

With bus service deregulation on the horizon, SBG undertook a major restructuring in 1985. The seven bus companies became 11 plus a coaching company. The plan was to align SBG operating companies with the Scottish regions, and only the Fife company escaped major surgery as its operating area aligned with the boundaries of Fife Region.

The SBG companies had undergone a name change in the late 1970s to a common style, retaining the geographical name, so Central, Eastern, Fife, Highland, Midland, Northern, and Western had Scottish Omnibuses Ltd added to their legal names, with new logos to a standard style; unlike NBC, there was no move to standard liveries.

The 1985 restructure added four more bus-operating companies

into the mix. Clydeside was formed from Western's northern area; Kelvin from parts of Central and Midland (the latter including east Glasgow routes transferred earlier in the year from Eastern Scottish); Lowland from Eastern's Borders and East Lothian area; and Strathtay from parts of Midland and Northern. Eastern also lost a depot each to Central and Midland, while Highland and Western's territorially isolated

LEFT: SBG's original Daimler Fleetline, Alexander-bodied Eastern Scottish DD961 (9961 SF) of 1963, in its final role as a survey bus for the Scotmap programme, gathering information in Glasgow in October 1980 with the aid of cartoon character Philippa Form. This bus was ordered by Baxter's of Airdrie and delivered to Scottish Omnibuses; it was rebodied in 1966 after a fire the previous year.
IAIN MacGREGOR

LEFT: An early product of the Scotmap exercise was to link Central SMT's hitherto separate Lanarkshire and Dunbartonshire networks into cross-Glasgow services catering for the needs of students and office workers. D2 (TYS 255M), a Dennis Dominator with Alexander RL body, was new in 1981 when photographed in East Kilbride new town south-east of Glasgow at the start of such a journey to Clydebank to the west of the city. Central was the first SBG subsidiary to buy Dominators.
GAVIN BOOTH

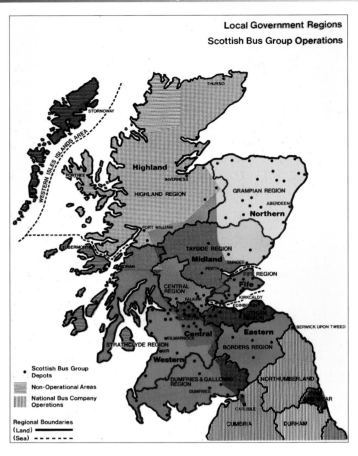

Local Government Regions
Scottish Bus Group Operations

• Scottish Bus Group Depots
▦ Non-Operational Areas
▥ National Bus Company Operations

Regional Boundaries
(Land) ———
(Sea) ------

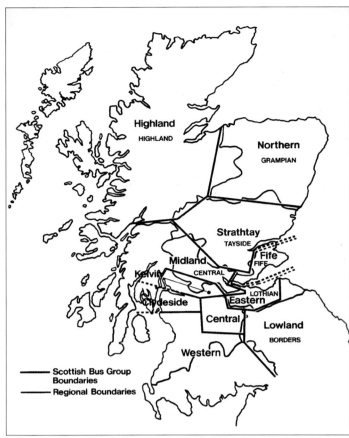

——— Scottish Bus Group Boundaries
——— Regional Boundaries

ABOVE LEFT AND ABOVE RIGHT: SBG produced these maps in 1975 and 1985 to overlay its subsidiaries' operating territories on the boundaries of the regional councils. The colour map is from 1975, showing considerable overlap in Strathclyde and Tayside, anomalies that were substantially reduced when the black and white map was produced ten years later.

operations in Argyll transferred to Midland.

The new companies adopted striking liveries. Clydeside went for red and yellow, Kelvin for blue and yellow, Lowland for green and yellow, and Strathtay for blue and marigold. Actual shades and applications changed over the years. The Clydeside, Kelvin and Strathtay companies also took up the competitive gauntlet by reintroducing conductor operation using former London Routemasters, which were faster and nippier than the buses the group normally used. Clydeside and Kelvin went into battle in Glasgow with Strathclyde Buses, using Routemasters and minibuses, while Strathclyde extended into what had previously been SBG territory.

Vehicular variety
The Routemasters and minibuses were not the only types new to SBG. In 1970, the group was sticking to a fairly conservative diet of single-deck and double-deck buses. Leyland Leopards with Alexander Y-type bodies seemed to be universal – the group bought over 2,800 Y-types – and

the Daimler Fleetline was the double-deck choice, usually with Alexander or ECW bodywork, but Western had a historic fondness for Northern Counties bodies.

There soon were Leopards too with the Alexander T-type 49-seat dual-purpose body, and from 1977 with Duple Dominant coach bodies. And Western had bucked the trend with an order for Volvo B58s with Alexander M-type bodies for its Glasgow-London services.

But the Fleetline was not the only show in town; SBG had never bought new Leyland Atlanteans, and had quickly rid itself of its troublesome Bristol VRTs, but three new types made their first appearance during the decade – the Dennis Dominator, MCW Metrobus and Volvo Ailsa. The Dominator and Metrobus gave SBG engineers their favourite Gardner engines, but the Scottish-built Ailsa was a different animal altogether, born out of SBG's desire for a front-engined model. The Fife company was the very first customer for production models of the Ailsa and other group companies followed this lead.

Two new single-deck bus models challenged the Leopard's dominance, the Leyland National and the Seddon Pennine 7. SBG had steered clear of the National until 1977 when Eastern bought a batch when it urgently needed new buses, and all group companies except Western subsequently bought Nationals. The Pennine 7 was created out of SBG's desire for a Gardner-engined Leopard, something Leyland would not provide. Eastern and Western went on to build up a fleet of these with Alexander T and Y type bodies and, for Eastern, Plaxton Supreme coach bodies.

SBG continued to buy Leyland Leopards until 1982, including a batch of 12m long models with Alexander M-type bodies for Scotland-London services. And there were new lighter-weight single-deck models for most fleets, in theory for less demanding routes. Ford's R1014

and R1114 chassis were popular from 1972, with Alexander bus and Duple coach bodies, although Eastern went for Bedford Y-series with Alexander bodies from 1971. Central and Western pointedly stuck to heavyweight chassis.

In the 1980s SBG was forced to consider different types as Leyland introduced new models to replace the Fleetline and Leopard. The Fleetline's replacement was the Olympian, and SBG received one of the very first. Similarly, when the

ABOVE: The original livery for the new Lowland Scottish company was light green and yellow, but the light green was soon replaced by a darker shade. This Leyland National, transferred from Eastern Scottish at the company's formation in 1985, was outside Galashiels depot, which also housed the new company's head office. GAVIN BOOTH

LEFT: Clydeside's competitive approach included the use of former London Routemasters on services in and around Glasgow. This is RM207 in July 1987 with the 'Hop on' logos at the front. Close behind is an Alexander-bodied Volvo Ailsa of Strathclyde Buses. GAVIN BOOTH

RIGHT: Kelvin
Scottish ordered
Mercedes-Benz
L608D minibuses
with 21-seat
Alexander bodies
and this one is
outside Glasgow's
Buchanan bus
station in July 1986
for inspection
by management.
GAVIN BOOTH

RIGHT: Strathtay
bought six
ex-Greater
Manchester
Transport Leyland
Fleetlines with
Northern Counties
bodies in 1987.
SD17 (LJA 476P)
was operating a
cross-city service
in Dundee that
year, in competition
with council-
owned Tayside
Public Transport.
IAIN MacGREGOR

Tiger was introduced to replace the Leopard, an SBG example was one of the launch vehicles. Leyland recognised the value of SBG business, particularly when new models were springing up to challenge what had been Leyland's near-monopoly.

The Dennis Dorchester was another heavyweight Gardner mid-engined chassis, supplied to Central, Clydeside and Western with Alexander and Plaxton bodies, but Leyland's Tiger proved to be the more popular choice, with Alexander, Duple and Plaxton bodies, and Leyland eventually made it available with the option of a Gardner engine. Western favoured Volvo's B10M for its coaches with Berkhof, Duple and Plaxton bodies, as well as Scania/Plaxton double-deckers.

SBG was the first customer for MCW's Metroliner double-deck coach and bought small numbers of integral Duple 425, MCW Metroliner and Leyland Royal Tiger Doyen single-deck coaches.

There were new double-deck models in evidence. Leyland Olympians with Alexander and ECW bodies, and Dennis Dominators and MCW Metrobuses with Alexander bodies. Volvo's mid-engined Citybus was another choice, as well as its rarer Leyland equivalent, the Lion.

Bus deregulation had prompted the purchase of the ex-London Routemasters, as well as a voyage

This former Central Scottish Volvo Ailsa with Alexander body had been transferred to Eastern Scottish by October 1988 as its VV45 (BGG 255S). This shows it in Edinburgh's Princes Street, still in Central colours, on a city service competing with Lothian Region Transport's red and white fleet. Behind is an Eastern Renault Dodge S56 with Alexander body with City Sprinter branding for another competing service. GAVIN BOOTH

Scottish Bus Group Fleet Sizes in the 1980s

	1984	1985	1989
Central	487	490	492
Clydeside		350	
Eastern	602	371	391
Fife	297	311	300
Highland	230	209	145
Kelvin		375	
Lowland		105	120
Midland	555	292	280
Northern	329	281	209
Strathtay		133	167
Western	688	337	661
TOTAL	**3,188**	**3,254**	**2,765**

These figures show the fleet sizes of SBG companies in 1984, before the major restructure; in 1985, following the restructure; and in 1989 as they were offered for sale at the time of privatisation.

Comparable figures for 1959, before the Alexander empire was split into three, show that Alexander had 1,933 vehicles, Western 1,100, Scottish Omnibuses (later Eastern) 783, Central 625 and Highland 156 – a total of 4,497 vehicles.

The numbers had dropped significantly by 1984, and the restructure of 1985 meant that Central had the largest fleet at 492, with significantly fewer vehicles at Eastern, Midland and Western following the creation of the four new companies – notably Clydeside and Kelvin with 725 buses between them.

By the time of the sale ,Western had grown again with the return of Clydeside territory, but the merging of Central and Kelvin made little difference to the combined Kelvin Central fleet total following drastic fleet reductions at each company.

LEFT:
The Central and Kelvin companies were merged in 1989 to create Kelvin Central Buses, in hopes of creating a more viable business to sell. By September 1990, Alexander RL-bodied Leyland Olympian 1821 (C114 BTS), new to Strathtay, was in the new red and cream livery which owed everything to Central's colours and nothing to Kelvin's blue and yellow. KCB was sold to its management and employees in 1991 and was acquired by Strathclyde Buses in 1994.
IAIN MacGREGOR

into the unknown territory of minibuses. The Renault Dodge S56 with Alexander body was the most popular choice, and there were Mercedes-Benz L608Ds for Kelvin. Lowland specified Reeve Burgess-bodied Bedford VAS5s for its Border Courier network — a service that combined the transport of people and medical supplies — and Midland bought Freight Rover Sherpas and MCW Metroriders.

Besides the Routemasters, SBG bought former London DMS-type and ex-West Midlands PTE Fleetlines for Western and ex-South Yorkshire PTE Van Hool McArdle-bodied Ailsas for Eastern

Privatisation
Added to the challenges of bus deregulation in 1986 was the uncertainty surrounding the future shape and ownership of SBG. Privatisation of the National Bus Company's (NBC) subsidiaries had fired the starting gun for the growth of new groups, including Stagecoach, that would survive to dominate the industry for the next three decades.

When the privatisation of SBG was announced early in 1988, the group mounted a campaign to stay as a single unit with some form of management/employee buy-out. This, it argued, would keep control in Scotland, but to no avail. Later that year it was announced that the group would be broken up and sold off in 11 units – the existing Eastern, Fife, Highland,

Lowland, Midland, Northern and Strathtay companies, plus the SBG Engineering and Scottish Citylink companies; SBG ultimately lost the Glasgow bus war and Clydeside was reunited with Western while Kelvin was combined with Central. SBG Engineering was closed.

Potential buyers waiting in the wings had to wait until 1990 before the sales process got underway, and it was completed in 1991. Five group companies went initially to management/employee buyouts, Midland to Grampian (a foundation stone of today's First Bus), Fife and Northern to Stagecoach, Strathtay to Yorkshire Traction and Highland to a joint bid from local operator Rapsons and the management buyout team at Citylink. The management buyout at Western sold Clydeside immediately to its employees.

Ironically, the sell-off had achieved one of SBG's stated aims – to keep control in Scotland; Yorkshire Traction

was the only successful English bidder. But as with the NBC sell-off, the situation did not survive for long and within a few years First and Stagecoach, both Scottish-based companies, controlled six of the former SBG companies between them, and this, added to First's strength with the former municipal fleets in Aberdeen and Glasgow, changed the Scottish bus landscape forever...or at least until the next reorganisation.

By 2022, Stagecoach owned the former Highland, Northern, Strathtay and Western businesses, while First's Glasgow business included what had been Kelvin Central and part of Clydeside. It had owned the Midland, Eastern and Lowland operations, but by September 2022 had sold or closed them down, with West Coast Motors' Borders Buses, McGill's and council-owned Lothian taking its place. McGill's had already bought the former Clydeside business as Arriva gradually exited Scotland. •

BELOW: Clydeside was merged back with Western in 1989, retaining its name on Western's final livery of black, white, grey and red, as on JR378 (LMS 158W), an Alexander-bodied Leyland Fleetline new to Midland and one of several Fleetlines acquired to replace its ex-London Routemasters. Western was the last SBG company to be sold in 1991. It was bought by its management and employees, but Clydeside was separated again and sold to its employees.
IAIN MacGREGOR

Smart thinking
for coaches

SBG relaunched and expanded its express coach business in 1983 with a brand that stood out and continues to thrive in new hands almost 40 years later. GAVIN BOOTH was involved in its birth and tells the story of how it came together.

Back in 1983, I was a member of Scottish Bus Group's (SBG) Express Services Working Party, a group of managers brought together to address the challenges that coach deregulation had brought us in 1980.

Looking back at what we had been offering at the start of 1980, it was clear something had to be done, but it is fair to say that there was a reluctance among our operating companies to lose outward ownership of the long-distance routes they had created.

For a start, the word "express" was a bit of a misnomer. For passengers it was a trade-off between fares that were lower than train travel and routes that were often bottom-numbingly long as they served many communities en route and usually included meal and toilet breaks.

In the 1970s. the 160 miles between Glasgow and Aberdeen took 6hr 1min – typically precise SBG timings – including a toilet stop at Perth and a 40min refreshment stop at Dundee. If you travelled all the way between Aberdeen and Corby, and people did because there are strong Scottish links with Corby, you could be stuck on a coach for 14hr 15min, although there were two 30min meal breaks. Edinburgh-Manchester, jointly with National Travel, took over 7hr.

We watched what was happening following the creation of National Express and in 1976 we had taken the bold step of creating a distinctive blue/white livery with prominent SCOTTISH branding for all of our prestigious Scotland-London services using fleets of dedicated vehicles with proper reclining seats and toilets. The main routes to London were from Edinburgh and Glasgow, operated by the SBG's Eastern and Western companies.

Most other services within Scotland and across the border into England used coaches at best, sometimes the group's beloved dual-purpose vehicles, and when stretched on a summer Saturday, literally anything that was to hand.

These routes were operated by the geographically appropriate

SBG companies, and on most cross-border services with various National Bus Company (NBC) companies. All-year cross-border services had historically been run jointly with English operators – principally Ribble on services to north-west England and United to the north-east. Some of our cross-border services were summer bucket-and-spade services that only carried Scottish-originating passengers.

These were seasonal, aimed squarely at Scottish holidaymakers and operated solely by SBG companies, although a reciprocal agreement allowed the use of NBC facilities for garaging, fuel and, occasionally, replacement vehicles following a breakdown. These carried holidaymakers to resorts like Blackpool and Scarborough, and even as far south as Bournemouth. Passengers travelled down on a Saturday to stay at the resort for a week or a fortnight, and were brought back on a Sunday by the coach that had arrived the previous day.

NBC's creation of National Express had led to much head-scratching at SBG's Edinburgh headquarters, but we still resisted the temptation to go down the NBC route of a standard livery for all of our long-distance routes. Not, that is, until National Express suggested to us that SBG might wish to bring its long-distance services into line under the National Express banner to create a truly national network. If anything was going to prod SBG managers into action, it was the threat of being told what to do by an English company. Hence

the creation of SBG's Express Services Working Party.

New competitors

This was the situation the working party addressed in 1983, prompted by the appearance of competition on internal and cross-border services. We estimated that what was at stake was our 1982 express revenue of £7.5million (the equivalent of £40.5million in 2022 terms), and that already £3million (£16.2million in 2022) had been won by competitors on what we had previously regarded as "our" corridors.

There was British Coachways, the ambitious but short-lived consortium of generally large private coach operators, and there was the long-established Glasgow-based Cotters, which had introduced an up-market service to London using coaches fitted with video and using hostesses to provide snacks and drinks.

But the greatest threat came from a new company called Stagecoach, which quickly

identified SBG's weaknesses and built up a network of strategic routes within Scotland and on to London. Stagecoach invested in brightly-painted Neoplan Skyliner double-deck coaches, and with a good, fast service at low fares, appealed to the very mobile student and youth markets.

The Express Services Working Party summed up our objectives as "improving and securing the group's overall financial position on express services while obtaining increased market share". Passenger surveys revealed that coach travel was perceived as the best value for money – but Stagecoach was seen as the best value of all; SBG's brand-image was weak while Stagecoach's was strong; passengers wanted reclining seats, toilets and good heating/ventilation; and snacks and videos were fine, but not essential.

From the start, we identified a need for a coordinated and recognisable product. The routes would still be operated by individual group companies but they had to be speeded up, and the coaches used had to reach a certain minimum standard, with reclining seats and toilets for journeys over 2hr. They had to be suitable for motorway operation, which debarred certain of the lighter-weight models beloved of some group fleets. What we then needed was a brand name and a livery.

A beauty contest

Choosing the name and livery involved a beauty parade in the

ABOVE: Before launching Citylink, SBG applied this livery to its first double-deck coaches. This was MCW Metroliner demonstrator TSX 1Y, which later became NDM1 in the Northern Scottish fleet, with a bagpiper escorting it out of Buchanan bus station in Glasgow on its inaugural run to London in March 1983. GAVIN BOOTH

LEFT: This was the Cityliner branding that was mooted as an alternative to Citylink, applied to Alexander T-type Leylands from the Midland and Fife fleets; another red and grey version was also applied to a Western SMT Volvo B58 with Alexander M-type body, the back of which is on the right. SBG used the Cityliner branding later for some shorter commuter services that were not part of the Citylink network. GAVIN BOOTH

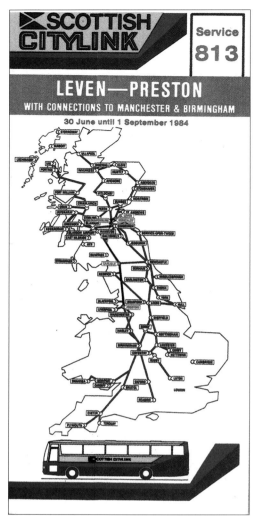

**RIGHT: This was
the first attempt
at a Citylink livery
in 1983, applied to
Eastern Scottish
YL321 (TFS 321Y),
a new Leyland
Tiger with Plaxton
Paramount body.
The fleetname
was redesigned
before Citylink was
launched later in the
year. The Western
SMT Volvo B58 in
the experimental
Cityliner livery
is behind.**
GAVIN BOOTH

Eastern Scottish New Street depot in Edinburgh where four coaches were inspected by senior managers. Three were in a white/grey livery with stripes reflecting the bus company's livery, and carried the brand Cityliner.

But one was blue/yellow and branded Scottish Citylink and this became the preferred livery, interpreted in a wide variety of ways by independently minded SBG managers who jealously protected their individual company identities. Although the livery application changed over the subsequent 40 years, it is still a recognisable blue/yellow scheme today.

Fares for the new Scottish Citylink services had to be competitive, easy to understand, relevant to different market segments, and tickets had to be easy to buy. And although individual group companies still operated the new Citylink network, and they retained the revenue from these routes, there was a need to get away from our current admin system, which could be cumbersome with a slow response speed.

When SBG reorganised from seven to 11 operating companies in 1985, a 12th company was created, Scottish Citylink Coaches, which managed, planned and marketed the network, and also accepted the risk and kept the revenue, paying operating companies on the basis of agreed mileage, which allowed the bus-operating companies to concentrate their management efforts on the forthcoming local bus service deregulation.

So in October 1983 the Scottish Citylink brand was launched, with a growing fleet of coaches in the new livery and racks full of colourful route leaflets supporting the concept and the image. The result was greater exposure to the public and the gradual acceptance of the brand; the fact that there is still a successful Scottish Citylink network today suggests that we may well have got things right in 1983.

Comparing the number of daily departures, single fares and fastest timings on a sample of routes in pre-deregulation 1980 with Scottish Citylink 1987, some routes were more frequent, but not all; some were more expensive, but not all; and most were considerably faster.

Glasgow-Manchester had jumped from two 1980 daily departures to five up-market Rapides in 1987, single fares were up from £7.80 to £12.50, but the fastest time was now 3hr 55min (1980 8hr 24min).

Edinburgh-Inverness was greatly improved by 1987, with seven departures daily (one at weekends in 1980); competition meant that single fares had dropped from £7.20 to £7 and timings had improved from a leisurely 5hr 20min to a more competitive 3hr 50min. The Edinburgh-Glasgow express

service had grown dramatically from 10 daily departures in 1980 to 33 in 1987, with single fares up from £1.80 to £2.25 but timings had improved from 1hr 40min to 1hr 10min.

Proper coaches

From the late 1970s, SBG companies had started to invest in proper coaches. They had previously relied heavily on dual-purpose vehicles, either bus shells with better seats or Alexander T-type bodies, more coach-like but often to be found on local bus duties. During the late 1970s, there had been deliveries of Duple Dominant-bodied Leyland Leopards for SBG's Fife, Highland, Midland and Northern fleets, and Plaxton Supreme-bodied Seddon Pennine 7s for Eastern, and these came in very handy in the deregulated 1980s.

But there was now a pressing need to beef up the group's coach fleet and a buying frenzy in the early 1980s brought a range of new products into group fleets – Leyland's new Tiger was a popular choice with a range of Duple and Plaxton bodies, as well as Leyland's new Royal Tiger Doyen. There were small batches of MCW's single-deck and double-deck Metroliner coaches, and Western went for Volvo B10Ms and Dennis Dorchesters.

By 1985 there were 219 coaches in Citylink livery, 142 with toilets, and a further 205 in company livery that were deemed suitable for Citylink duplication. The Citylink-liveried coaches

were Dennis Dorchesters, Leylands (Leopards, Tigers and Royal Tiger Doyens), MCW single-deck and double-deck Metroliners, Seddon Pennine 7s and Van Hools (Alicrons, Alizées and Astrals). Bodywork was mostly by Alexander, Duple and Plaxton plus a few Berkhofs and the Van Hools. The company-liveried offerings were more straightforward – Dennis, Leyland and Seddon models with Alexander, Duple and Plaxton bodies.

There was more upheaval ahead. SBG's subsidiaries were privatised in 1990/91, with a management buyout acquiring Scottish Citylink in 1990. It was sold on to National Express three years later and to Metroline, which was bought by ComfortDelGro, in 2000. By this time Stagecoach had established a strong presence in Scotland through acquisitions and expansion and had developed a network of express services throughout the country. This led to the current joint venture between Stagecoach and ComfortDelGro in 2005.

Scottish Citylink still has a strong presence in Scotland, operating a network that links the major cities with each other and with Campbeltown, Fort William, Oban and Skye, all destinations on Scotland's west coast, using a fleet of impressive coaches, often three-axle and double-deck, which highlight how far the Scottish Citylink brand has come in nearly 40 years. And it is good to see that our working party meetings all these years ago still bear fruit. •

LEFT: Citylink branding in March 1984 on the backs of a Duple Laser-bodied Leyland Tiger in the Highland fleet and a Western SMT Seddon Pennine 7 with Alexander T-type body.
GAVIN BOOTH

MIDDLE: The Citylink network included the Edinburgh-Glasgow motorway express service, one of SBG's few all-year internal Scottish expresses before 1980. It was numbered X14 when this Plaxton Paramount-bodied Tiger of Eastern Scottish was loading in Glasgow in November 1983, later became the 500 and today is numbered 900. It began in the early 1950s when the main section of inter-city road was a deadly three-lane single carriageway with shared central overtaking lane.
GAVIN BOOTH

BOTTOM: By 1988, operators other than SBG subsidiaries were also working with Citylink. One of the more exotic coaches in the familiar livery then was this Volvo B10M operated by Dodds of Troon, with Italian-made Padane ZX body.
GAVIN BOOTH

Flagships for the flagship

ABOVE: Eastern Scottish painted its Alexander M-types in a primrose and black livery that set them apart from the operator's standard green and cream. Here, three of its 1970 delivery of Bristol REMH6Gs are loading in Edinburgh bus station on an August evening. Their destination displays were reversible illuminated boards. IAIN MacGREGOR

For decades, the coaches operated on the mainly overnight services linking Scotland with London were built to a higher standard of luxury than most others anywhere in Britain, a status maintained with the advent of the Alexander M-type in 1968. DAVID TOY tells their story, with some additional information from GAVIN BOOTH and ALAN MILLAR.

The mainly overnight coach service between Scotland and London — Scottish Omnibuses (Eastern Scottish) from Edinburgh and Western SMT from Glasgow — was the Scottish Bus Group's (SBG) flagship operation which justified the development of a new generation of premium luxury coaches at the end of the 1960s.

These had been running since the late 1920s, with Scotch Corner on the A1 Great North Road the point where the convoys of southbound coaches converged

and northbound ones diverged, with the Glasgow service following the A66, A6 and A74 to reach Scotland's largest city while the Edinburgh route continued to the capital on the A1, A697 and A68, crossing the border at Coldstream.

The overnight service ran all year, supplemented by a summer daytime operation, with stops when required at many of the old coaching towns along the A1, like Hatfield, Stevenage, Baldock, Biggleswade, Stamford, Grantham, Newark, Doncaster, Wetherby and Boroughbridge. In 1937, SMT's service to/from Edinburgh was scheduled to take

15hr 19min, while Western SMT's to/from Glasgow was booked for an equally precise 15hr 53min.

It was little changed by 1960, other than that 1min had been added to the journey time to Glasgow. The return fare had risen from £2.50 to £4.20, which equates in 2021 values to a fall from £119 to £68. This was a premium service for well-heeled travellers, using coaches with comfortable seats and generous legroom, with blankets provided for overnight warmth.

By 1969, dual carriageways and motorway sections of the A1 had reduced the journey time.

And the main Glasgow-London service was re-routed by the M6 and M1 by 1972, with a non-stop service calling only at the Charnock Richard service area in Lancashire. By 1987, there were five daily departures on the Edinburgh-London service, compared with three in 1980. The single fare had risen from £11.50 to £14.50 (down from £40 to £34 at 2021 values), and the fastest timing was now 7hr 45m compared with 9hr. The service was faster and more frequent, but was priced for a more budget-conscious clientele.

Standards are raised

Toilets were fitted in new Alexander-bodied coaches purchased from 1951 onwards. AEC Regal IVs bought then had 30 seats, as did Guy Arab UF and LUF and Leyland Leopard coaches added to the Western SMT fleet until 1960. The increase in legal length limit to 36ft (11m) in 1961 allowed for 38 seats in Leopards for Western, AEC Reliances for Scottish Omnibuses and Bristol RELH6Gs delivered to both fleets in 1966 with 150hp Gardner 6HLX engines, manual gearboxes and underfloor luggage accommodation.

Each coach ran with two drivers and, between journeys, the coaches were parked at London Transport's Stockwell and Camberwell garages, where they were fuelled and cleaned ready for their return trip north. The SBG companies employed fitters based in London who travelled between the two garages and conducted any necessary repairs. If parts were not available, they were sent from Scotland on the next coach, though occasionally drivers forgot to hand over the required part and it arrived back home without being fitted.

Until the early 1980s, there also were long-established two-, three- and four-day summer routes between Edinburgh and London which were much more like extended tours and used higher capacity coaches.

The two-day east coast route operated three days a week with an overnight stop at York in both directions, the two-day west coast stopped overnight in Chester, while the three-day west coast also ran three days a week and stopped overnight at Bowness-on-Windermere and Stratford-upon-Avon in both directions. Operated just once a week were a three-day southbound-only east coast route with overnight stops at York and Cambridge and a four-day northbound with overnights in Stratford, Chester and Bowness.

Birth of the M-type

An opportunity for more change came with the increase in permitted length limit of coaches to 12m (39ft 4in) from February 1967, which allowed for up to 42 seats plus a rear toilet — still a rarity on British coaches — and either more overall capacity on the service or a reduced number of duplicate coaches.

Eastern Scottish general manager Roddie MacKenzie, who became SBG's executive director responsible for engineering in 1969, played a leading part in developing these coaches. He travelled to the United States to view the Greyhound network and the General Motors coaches it was using at the time, and in 1966/67 evaluated two rear-engined German integral vehicles on the Edinburgh-London service.

The first, for which the traffic commissioners granted dispensation to operate it, was a 38-seat 10m left-hand-drive Magirus-Deutz 150L10 with a 150hp 9.5litre air-cooled V6 9.5 engine and an eight-speed manual gearbox. The second was OLH 302E, an 11m 43-seat right-hand-drive Mercedes-Benz O302

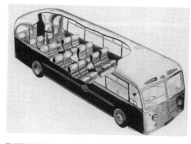

GLASGOW to LONDON

Single Fare 42/- Return £4 4 0

GO BY ROAD—RETURN BY RAIL £5 10 0

Book at WESTERN S.M.T. CO., LTD.
290 Buchanan Street, Glasgow
Phone : DOU 8634/5

with a 7.98litre engine rated at 175hp and air suspension.

SBG then worked with Alexander's coachworks to develop a bespoke coach based on a 20ft wheelbase 12m version of the Bristol RE, the REMH6G with 6HLX engine, semi-automatic gearbox and air suspension.

The aluminium body, which Alexander called the M-type, was designed for overnight travel and had the look of contemporary North American coaches. The side windows were small and double glazed, as these coaches would operate mainly in hours of darkness when passengers had little need to see out but needed to be kept warm. They were trapezoidal in shape and were spaced to match the reclining Chapman Leveroll seats. Each

ABOVE: Three of the Leyland Leopards with M-type bodies posed outside Alexander's Falkirk factory in spring 1975, left to right for Fife, Northern and Eastern Scottish. The three for Eastern were soon transferred to Fife and Northern, and all lost their separate liveries after the blue and white Scottish livery was introduced in 1976.
GAVIN BOOTH

RIGHT: Western SMT KV2535 (HSD 706N), one of the eight Volvo B58s with M-type bodies, preparing to leave Glasgow on the motorway service to London via the M6 and M1. The M-type Bristols were the first to have Western Scottish rather than plain Western fleetnames, raising awareness in London of where these services ran.
IAIN MacGREGOR

passenger had a reading light and an air vent.

The body sides were ribbed, insulation was sandwiched between the side and roof panels, and a Webasto oil-fired air heater supplemented the conventional two under-seat heaters during the low temperature nights. The floor was carpeted to provide further insulation, although in time these were difficult to keep clean. The passenger door hinged outwards. The driver's cab was lower than the passenger compartment and had a padded driver's seat and a rounded dash panel.

The front and back windscreens were the same as those on the Y-type, while the front mouldings — with destination display built into the roof dome — were from Alexander's W-type single-deck city bus body. Front and rear roof marker lights were an added touch that enhanced visibility at night. The side fleetnames — Eastern Scottish or Western Scottish — also were illuminated. Western SMT's M-types were its first vehicles with the word Scottish added to the fleetname. Eastern Scottish used reversible destination boards rather than blinds ('London from Edinburgh' on one side, 'Edinburgh from London' on the other), while Western fitted blinds.

A full-size mock-up was followed by a prototype exhibited at the Commercial Motor Show in London in September 1968 when it was one of the big talking points, drawing comparisons — some favourable — with another ground-breaking coach, the first of a fleet of 11m 60-seat ECW-bodied Bristol VRL double-deckers for Ribble subsidiary Standerwick's motorway services

between Lancashire and London. Unladen weight was 8ton 18cwt.

The show vehicle was the first of an eventual fleet of 33 for Eastern Scottish and introduced a black and primrose livery unique to these vehicles, one that helped distinguish them in London's Victoria Coach Station and at intermediate stops from Western's black and white counterparts, of which 37 were built by 1971.

Shown at the 1972 Commercial Motor Show, in the new National livery, was the only M-type for the National Bus Company (NBC) and the only one not ordered by SBG. It was operated initially by Ribble, had 46 seats plus a toilet, and was built on a 12m Leyland Leopard chassis, so had a mid-mounted rather than rear engine.

Leopards, Volvos and Seddons

SBG also bought 12 Leopards with M-type bodies and semi-automatic gearboxes in 1975 as it expanded the coverage of its overnight London services. By then, it had stopped buying Bristols for other work and found that the Gardner-engined REMHs lacked the power needed on sustained daytime motorway journeys. These also brought the additional refinement of an in-swinging door.

The first additional service had started in summer 1973, with the growth of the North Sea oil industry justifying the introduction of a 540mile Aberdeen-London service operated by Alexander (Midland) with four of Western's seven-year-old RELH6G 38-seaters. This linked Midland's existing Aberdeen-Glasgow summer express with Western's Glasgow-London route.

It proved sufficiently successful for Alexander (Northern) to apply (successfully) to operate

a through service from April 1974 onwards, initially with six black and white RELH6Gs hired from Western but with Northern Scottish fleetnames. It operated via Dundee, Perth and Stirling and was branded the Northern Scot. The coaches' fuel tanks were topped up at Midland's Bannockburn depot near Stirling on north and southbound journeys.

Eastern Scottish had extended Edinburgh-London journeys to start across the Forth Road Bridge in Dunfermline and Kirkcaldy, and this was extended farther into Fife to Glenrothes new town and was to be operated by Alexander (Fife).

The order for 12 Leopards was split three ways, six for Northern, three each for Fife and Eastern. They were delivered in the operators' liveries (Northern yellow and cream, Fife red and cream, Eastern black and primrose). Two of the Eastern coaches were soon transferred to Northern, while the third went to Fife and also was in the Northern fleet from 1979.

By 1974, the REMHs had accumulated high mileages and replacements were required for the front-line service. Leyland deliveries to customers had fallen back, with longer lead times. Nonetheless, it was a surprise in late 1974 when it was announced that Western had ordered eight Volvo B58-61 chassis with M-type bodies. These were SBG's first vehicles with imported chassis, bought at a time when there was still an expectation that public undertakings would buy British. The chassis had the Volvo 9.6litre TDH100A horizontal engine rated at 210hp, positioned amidships with a Volvo K19 five-speed manual gearbox.

They were delivered in April/May at the same time as one of the 1971 Bristols was rebodied after suffering extensive fire damage; SBG modified the REMHs around the same time to fit a roof-mounted air intake, a feature since new on the older RELHs. The Volvos returned fuel consumption of 10 to 10.5mpg, which was slightly lower than the Gardner-powered REMHs. These were Western's last new M-types and were once again in the black and white coach livery.

SBG introduced a group-wide corporate identity for the London services in March 1976, of blue and white with a large SCOTTISH fleetname in capital letters along with a logo based on the Saltire flag. An Eastern Scottish REMH was the first recipient and some of Western's Volvos also were among the first to be repainted. A smaller version of the fleetname and logo, accompanied by the subsidiary company's name, replaced traditional fleetnames on all SBG vehicles from late 1978.

The last M-types to be built, six Seddon Pennine 7s with mid-mounted Gardner 6HLXB engines and manual gearboxes, were delivered to Eastern Scottish in June 1976, painted in the new livery.

The Dominant III

Although it bought no more M-types, SBG's next generation of London coaches – delivered between 1981 and 1983 – also had trapezoid windows, a feature that also found brief favour on vehicles built for several other operators that were not intended for overnight travel.

Alexander's Falkirk factory was so busy developing and manufacturing double-deck bus bodies that it could not afford the time and resources to develop a new London service coach within SBG's timescale. The group turned instead to Duple in Blackpool to develop a variant of its Dominant body with trapezoid windows, toilet, 46 Fugelsang reclining seats trimmed in blue check moquette, and interior body sides, luggage racks and ceiling in two-tone blue moquette (the ceiling trim also was yellow) and a gold carpet.

It called this the Dominant III and offered it as an option on a variety of chassis, some far less luxuriously appointed and shorter than SBG's required 12m. Recently formed Stagecoach, which took advantage of coach deregulation to compete with SBG's London services from October 1980, was one of the first buyers of the new model.

SBG bought them on two of the latest mid-engined chassis with air suspension. Eastern Scottish received eight Leyland Tigers (the first was at the launch event for the new chassis in Morocco in March 1981) with 218hp TL11 engine and five-speed Hydracyclic semi-automatic gearbox. Western bought 12 on the Volvo B10M-61 with 242hp Volvo THD100C engine and a manual six-speed ZF S6-90 gearbox, with four more following in 1982.

Twenty-five others purchased in 1982/83 had the Dominant III version of Duple's new Goldliner body, a high-floor variant which increased the luggage capacity within the wheelbase. Two were

built on the B10M-61 chassis for Western, which also took four on Tiger chassis. There were ten more Tigers for Eastern Scottish and six for Alexander (Northern), followed in 1983 by three Tigers for Alexander (Fife).

The first of Northern's six — the only one with a six-speed ZF manual gearbox — was not for the London service, but was a replacement for an M-type Leopard that had become the team coach for the Aberdeen Football Club. This had a high standard of interior finish with tables and ornamental reading lights. To entertain the players, a stereo system, televisions and video equipment were fitted. At the rear there were full cooking facilities with a cool box in the boot fed by a 240v generator built in the side of the coach; a temporary bed could be laid at the rear. It was entered in the 1982 Brighton Coach Rally where it won awards for Best Leyland, Best Duple Coach and the coach that had travelled the farthest to the rally.

Duple discontinued the Dominant after that, and with it trapezoid windows no longer were available. SBG continued to purchase high-specification coaches for its London services from a variety of manufacturers and still had nine of the later M-types in the Eastern and Fife fleets when the group was restructured in June 1985. The steel-framed Dominant IIIs proved less enduring, with many requiring major rebuilding in which conventional glazing replaced the distinctive originals. •

BELOW LEFT: The six Seddon Pennine 7s for Eastern Scottish were the first M-types delivered in the blue and white Scottish livery which was introduced on Bristols in 1976. XS750 (MSF 750P) is now preserved.
ALAN MILLAR

BELOW RIGHT: Eastern Scottish XH553 (MSC 553X), Duple Dominant Goldliner III-bodied Leyland Tiger, when new in 1982.
GAVIN BOOTH

State-owned
in the capital

As **ALAN MILLAR** explains, London Transport went through two periods in state ownership, the first for 22 years and the second for ten years, while its green Country Area buses were state-owned for an unbroken period of over 30 years. Some of this change also impacted on other parts of the state-owned bus industry.

ABOVE: Hants & Dorset TD895 (HLJ 44), a lowbridge ECW-bodied Bristol K6A, was one of the 190 similar vehicles that Tilling companies lent to London Transport when new. It has been restored to the condition in which it operated in London.
CHRISTOPHER CARTER

State-owned buses served parts or all of London from January 1948 to January 1995, and over two lengthy periods — 1948 to 1969 and 1984 to 2000 — London Transport was by slightly different names a state-owned body.

The original London Passenger Transport Board of 1933 was something of a hybrid, a public board with a great deal of autonomy to go about its business as it wished, provided that the

books balanced; it was akin to the BBC. Together with the four main-line railways, it was placed in government control for the duration of World War Two in recognition of the part it was expected to play in the wider war effort and of the strategic importance of the entire British railway network.

Its status changed with the postwar Labour government's policy of bringing most transport into state ownership — what is generally described as nationalisation — and on New

Year's Day 1948 it became the London Transport Executive, one of the arms of the newly created British Transport Commission (BTC) which also oversaw the Railway, Road Transport, Docks & Inland Waterways and Hotels executives. For its first five years, the BTC's head office was within the London Transport headquarters building at 55 Broadway.

The BTC lasted until 1963, after which a London Transport Board succeeded the London Transport Executive, with the reconstituted

organisation reporting direct to the Ministry of Transport and ultimately to the minister.

The years in state control possibly frustrated London Transport, as the BTC had to balance London's needs and ambitions against those of its other spheres of activity, and especially of British Railways which was embarking on a massive modernisation programme that required capital investment that London Transport might have believed should have flowed its way instead. It took nearly 20 years, for instance, to secure funding and government approval for the Victoria line.

Not that London Transport was lacking in early postwar investment. It had already committed itself to the start of a huge fleet renewal programme before it came under BTC control, and by 1954 had taken delivery of over 7,600 vehicles including 6,805 AEC and Leyland double-deckers of its RT family. It had replaced its remaining trams between 1950 and 1952, and was leading the development of the Routemaster which initially would replace its large trolleybus fleet between 1959 and 1962. It also built several new bus garages and opened the Aldenham overhaul works in 1956 on a site in Hertfordshire originally intended as a branch of the Northern line.

One bit of tidying up within BTC took place in 1951 when Eastern National routes centred on Grays in Essex were transferred to London Transport's Country Area.

BTC to the rescue

Like much of the country, it suffered from early postwar shortages which were holding back the delivery of RTs while it struggled to keep some of its older vehicles in roadworthy condition. It hired coaches and drivers from private operators, but was able to prevail upon the BTC to bring the first visible sign of its involvement in London Transport on to the streets from late 1948 until May 1950.

That was when 190 brand new ECW-bodied Bristol K5G and K6A double-deckers intended for Tilling group fleets across England and south-west Scotland were lent to London Transport. There were green ones intended for Eastern National, Southern National, Western National, Southern Vectis, Hants & Dorset, United Counties and Crosville, red ones for Caledonian, Eastern Counties, United Automobile and Westcliff-on-Sea, and red and cream ones for Brighton Hove & District. Most had lowbridge

ABOVE: London Transport RLH48 (MXX 248), a lowbridge Weymann-bodied AEC Regent III preserved in Country Area green. This was one of the second batch ordered by London but which were almost identical to the 20 ordered by Midland General. ALAN WALLWORK

ABOVE: RFW13, one of the 15 ECW-bodied AEC Regal IV coaches delivered to London Transport in 1951.
IAIN MacGREGOR

bodies with a side sunken upper deck gangway; the 45 for Eastern Counties and Brighton Hove & District had 56-seat highbridge bodies.

They were allocated in small numbers to red bus garages, identified by a prominent London Transport name on the front and the organisation's bulls-eye roundel on the radiator.

They were not London Transport's first Bristol K double-deckers, as 29 K5Gs and K6As with Park Royal and Duple wartime utility bodies were delivered in 1942 and 1945 along with 435 utility Guys and 281 Daimlers. The 29 Bristols were sold within BTC after withdrawal in 1952/53, to Crosville, Lincolnshire Road Car, Brighton Hove & District and also to United Automobile which bought them on behalf of the municipal fleet in Hartlepool; many were fitted with replacement bodies after leaving London.

BTC also found an internal buyer for more than a quarter of the wartime Guy Arabs around the same time, selling 128 to its Scottish fleets which put all but 11 of them into service, several with new bodies. The commission also facilitated the sale of another 60 Arab chassis to Edinburgh Corporation, which modified them to carry new, wider bodies.

It is notable, however, that in 1955/56 when London Transport realised it had bought more RT family double-deckers than it now required, it sold the surplus examples to non-BTC operators through the Bird's dealership in Stratford-upon-Avon rather than to sister operators in the state sector.

Around the same time as the loaned Bristols arrived, the BTC found itself with spare buses on order that would help meet one of London Transport's more niche requirements. Midland General, one of the Balfour

Beatty companies taken over at the beginning of 1948, had 50 AEC Regent IIIs on order with lowbridge Weymann bodies, but apparently only required 30 of them. London Transport wanted to renew its entire fleet of lowbridge double-deckers and the 20 new Regents that apparently were no longer needed in the East Midlands were the closest it was likely to get to making a quick start on replacing those vehicles.

They were delivered in the summer of 1950 for use as green Country Area buses, forming the first 20 members of its RLH class. They differed from RTs by having the standard version of the Regent III chassis with a high bonnet line and radiator, and their bodies owed more to Midland General's requirements than London's. But they fulfilled the need and were followed in 1952 by another 56 of near identical design, some of which were red Central Area buses.

ECW's 100 bodies

As part of BTC, London Transport experienced some of the same pressure to place orders with Bristol and ECW as was already applied to the Tilling and Scottish companies. A trial of lightweight single-deckers pitched the AEC Monocoach and Leyland Tiger Cub against an ECW-bodied Bristol LS5G loaned by Bristol Tramways in 1952/53. The Bristol was tested on a long cross-London Green Line route and a local service in Reigate and was fitted for much of the trial with a non-standard semi-automatic gearbox.

No orders followed for any of the three types in that trial, and with 700 heavy-duty RF-class AEC Regal IVs delivered in 1951-53, the organisation had no need to buy many single-deckers for another 12 years.

It bought no Bristols of any sort during the period when the manufacturer was prevented from supplying third party customers,

but London Transport was persuaded to place orders with ECW for a total of precisely 100 bodies built largely to bespoke designs.

The first 15, ready for the Festival of Britain in 1951, were the RFW-class of 8ft wide Regal IV (6in wider than the RFs) private hire coaches with 39-seat bodies to a new design that may have been influenced by continental European practice; five similar vehicles were built around the same time for another state-owned London operator, the Tilling Transport coach business. Only those 20 were produced.

The biggest proportion of the 100 bodies were 84 GS-class 26-seat rural buses. These were built on a bonneted Guy Special chassis itself designed to meet London Transport's requirements and delivered during 1953. Their bodies blended ECW construction with London styling.

The 100th bore no resemblance to any other ECW product. This was CRL4, the fourth of four prototype Routemasters and the first built to coach standards for cross-London Green Line routes. In common with third prototype RML3 (built by Weymann), this had Leyland rather than the AEC running units in RM1, RM2 and all production vehicles. It was built in 1955/56 using drawings prepared by London Transport, Park Royal and AEC and was

delivered in February 1957, by which time London Transport had placed its first order for 650 production Routemasters with AEC and Park Royal.

London Transport was pleased with the quality of CRL4 and ECW was keen to build more Routemasters, albeit not in the quantities that Park Royal could achieve. The Country Area wanted another 50 for Green Line work in 1958, which was the sort of volume that the Lowestoft factory could have produced, but their purchase was delayed until the trolleybuses had all been replaced in 1962. Park Royal built 68 of them, the RMC class.

The birth of London Country

Local government reorganisation brought the first period of state ownership to an end and also ushered in the second period 14 years later. A two-tier system took effect in April 1965, with the Greater London Council (GLC) responsible for strategic matters that were intended to include transport, and 32 boroughs focused on matters more local. The GLC covered all of the area of the old London County Council along with most of Middlesex and parts of Essex, Hertfordshire, Kent and Surrey.

It became responsible for London Transport from January 1970, when the organisation once

BELOW: ECW's main contribution to the London Transport bus fleet was to build the bodies on the 84-strong GS class of Guy Specials, 26-seaters built for quiet rural routes.
ALAN MILLAR

again was named the London Transport Executive. Except not all of London Transport left state ownership. The red Central Area buses and the Underground did, including a few bus routes and outer sections of Underground lines that extended into surrounding counties.

The green Country Area buses and Green Line coach services fell largely outside the GLC area, though most Green Line routes ran into and often across central London and therefore clocked up most of their mileage within the strategic council's area. Several green bus routes also served population centres like Croydon which were firmly within Greater London. The 28 garages at which they were based, however, were in the surrounding counties where most green buses ran.

The solution was to keep these operations in state ownership, transferring the garages, routes and 1,267 buses to a new subsidiary of the National Bus Company (NBC), London Country Bus Services. Its head office was in Reigate towards the southern end of a sprawling operating territory that covered parts of Essex, Hertfordshire, Bedfordshire, Buckinghamshire, Berkshire, Surrey, Sussex and Kent. It adjoined areas served by six NBC companies, Eastern National, United Counties, Thames Valley, Aldershot & District, Southdown and Maidstone & District.

Without understanding all the facts, it is tempting to imagine that NBC could have split the Country Area in six and bolted parts on to the territories of those existing companies. That ignores some fundamentals. The culture, pay and conditions, operating practices and fleet content at London Country were more akin to London Transport than any of those other NBC companies. London Transport had focused more investment on the red buses, so nearly three quarters of the London Country fleet in 1970 was at least 16 years old, over-age by bus industry standards. It remained heavily dependent on London Transport for engineering support to maintain over 900 elderly AECs.

One territorial change was to transfer some Southdown routes in Crawley new town to London Country, which later in the 1970s also took over some routes in Gravesend.

In the early years, NBC diverted resources into London Country to accelerate the updating of its fleet, starting in 1971 with 15 AEC Swifts from South Wales Transport and the diversion of an outstanding order for 21 more Swifts from South Wales which arrived in 1972. Major investment in double-deckers was boosted with 30 new Leyland Atlanteans intended for Midland Red and 11 Daimler Fleetlines ordered by Western Welsh.

London Country gradually took on the outward appearance of an NBC company by applying its corporate identity and advertising to a fleet that by 1973 was composed increasingly of standard NBC vehicles like the Leyland National, Park Royal-bodied Leyland Atlantean and ECW-bodied Bristol LHS. These were supplemented in 1975/76 by three Leyland Titan PD3 double-deckers acquired from Southdown.

The Green Line network, compromised by increasing traffic congestion, was rationalised from 1977 with an investment in new coaches offering better comfort for longer distance riders than on the ordinary service buses used beforehand. The inheritance of ex-London Transport vehicles finally ended in March 1980 when the last Routemasters were

withdrawn and sold back to their original owner.

State control and tendering

Control of the GLC changed at every election, alternating between the Labour and Conservative parties. If the Conservatives were in government, then Labour won the most seats on the GLC; if Labour was in government, the Conservatives took control at County Hall. It was a classic example of a protest vote.

Labour formed the administration of the 1965-67 GLC, winning in 1964 a few months before it won the general election with a tiny majority. The Conservatives won in 1967, Labour in 1973, the Conservatives in 1977 and Labour in 1981, forming a radical administration that locked political horns with Margaret Thatcher's Conservative government with policies that included heavily subsidised cheap bus and Underground fares.

Her government abolished the GLC and its six counterparts in other English city regions from 1986, but the GLC had lost its responsibility for transport two years earlier with the creation of a new state-owned body, London Regional Transport, responsible for public transport, roads and other areas of GLC responsibility. Despite the name change, the outward trading name remained London Transport.

London Buses and London Underground were established as companies in overall charge of direct transport operations and a process of putting bus routes out to competitive tender began on a relatively small scale in 1985 and gradually gained pace. By the early 1980s, neighbouring counties like Surrey were reducing the cost of subsidising red London Transport bus routes that crossed their boundaries by securing similar levels of service from operators with lower costs, London Country among them.

The award of the first of London Transport's tendered service rounds in 1985 set a pattern of what was to follow. Out of 12 routes, six were retained by London Buses, two went to independent coach operators and two each to NBC subsidiaries Eastern National and London Country. The routes had been selected in part because London Transport knew there were operators with garage space within reasonable reach of one terminus.

Both NBC operators went on to win more contracts over the next couple of years, with London Country sourcing secondhand Atlanteans from within and beyond NBC to meet these extra commitments. Other operators made gains too, but in many cases green state-owned buses replaced apparently more expensive red ones.

Privatisation programmes

London Country was managed separately from NBC's southern region, so was not split into smaller companies when most of the others were. But in preparation for privatisation, to make the business more attractive to private sector buyers, that finally happened in September 1986 with the creation of four companies, London Country Bus (North East), London Country Bus (North West), London Country Bus (South West) and London Country Bus (South East). The central workshops in Crawley were vested with a separate company, Gatwick Engineering. The South East company soon renamed itself Kentish Bus.

All five companies were sold towards the end of the NBC privatisation programme, between January and March 1988.

London Buses also was being prepared for privatisation and the possible deregulation of London bus services, which in the event did not happen. It had already established a lower cost subsidiary, Westlink, to compete for tendered service contracts in south-west London, and in April 1989 the rest of the operation was restructured into 11 companies: East London, London Forest, Leaside, London Northern, Metroline, CentreWest, London United, London General, South London, London Central and Selkent. The round-London sightseeing operation became London Coaches.

Tendering losses led to the closure of London Forest and the transfer of parts of its business to East London and Leaside, and the transfer of Bexleyheath garage from Selkent to London Central.

Privatisation began in the summer of 1994, with CentreWest the first to be sold, and ended in early January 1995 with the sale of the South London company. State-owned bus operation in London had finished after 47 years. London Regional Transport lived on until 2000, replaced by Transport for London, a body that reports to the elected mayor of London. •

BELOW: After it was privatised, Eastern National continued to win contracts to provide tendered services for London Transport, and in July 1990 was operating Woodford Hoppa service W13. TERRY BLACKMAN

The sole public
sector survivor

Buses in Northern Ireland have been in state ownership since 1935 and have not been privatised. Operations were restructured at Ulsterbus, and PAUL SAVAGE explains how the new company was affected by all that was going on in the province in the 1970s and 1980s.

ABOVE: The secondhand Leylands acquired for the start of Ulsterbus operations included 48 Weymann-bodied Tiger Cubs from Edinburgh Corporation, rendered surplus by the conversion of a busy circular route to double-deckers. This was 9315 (SWS 15) in Kings Road, Belfast in June 1968.
IAIN MacGREGOR

Ulsterbus came into being on April 17, 1967 when it took over most of the bus operations of the Ulster Transport Authority (UTA), the province's buses having been in state ownership since 1935. Today it and sister company Metro are the UK's only state-owned bus operators.

Besides Ulsterbus, Belfast Corporation continued to operate the services within the city, while a few UTA routes were taken over by Sureline Coaches of Lurgan and Coastal Bus Service of Portrush. The Unionist government at Stormont had hoped to involve more of the private sector in this separation of buses, road freight and greatly reduced railway lines.

In charge of the new company was one of the most remarkable bus industry executives of the time. When appointed managing director (designate) in 1965, Werner Wolfgang Heubeck was 42 and had no experience or qualifications relating to the public transport industry, no connection with Northern Ireland and his employment at the time was as manager at a paper mill near Aberdeen.

He was born in Germany, conscripted into military service in 1942 and taken to the United States as a prisoner of war in 1943. While working as an interpreter at the war crimes trials in his home city of Nuremburg in 1946, he met his Welsh future wife and settled in Britain three years later. Having almost accidentally seen the advertisement for the Ulsterbus job, he prepared for the successful interview by spending a day with the local bus manager in Aberdeen and a weekend visiting Ulster.

One of his first tasks was a comparison between the UTA's road passenger services and those of the Scottish Bus Group (SBG), which indicated that UTA bus revenues were comparable, but costs were higher. Fares were higher in Northern Ireland and offpeak utilisation of vehicles was substantially lower, partly because of a big commitment to schools services. He also concluded that apparent losses on the bus side were mostly attributable to cost allocations from elsewhere in the UTA, charges which would disappear with the creation of the new company, so making it a viable prospect.

He concluded that changes, such as greater efficiency and one-man operation, were needed. Despite suspicion, even hostility, from staff and unions, issues were overcome and his firmness, fairness and decency earned him the respect and loyalty of most staff.

The Ulsterbus company was registered on June 1, 1966, followed on July 25 by the registration of a subsidiary business, Ulster Coach Tours, to look after daily and extended coach tours. The UTA had already changed its livery from two-tone green and cream to eau de nil (a light greenish blue) and cream. Ulsterbus made a more radical change to riviera blue and trader ivory, and the UTA revealed it in the metal on December 7 that year on one of 48 Weymann-bodied Leyland Tiger Cubs acquired from Edinburgh Corporation.

These had been new in 1959 and were no longer required in Edinburgh after roads were lowered under railway bridges on one of the city's busiest routes. The UTA was unable to invest in new vehicles while the transition to Ulsterbus took place and these were the biggest part of a purchase of 108 secondhand Leyland single-deckers. There also were 38 Leyland-bodied Royal Tigers and seven Weymann-bodied Olympics from Ribble and 15 Alexander-bodied Leopard L1 coaches from Western SMT, which had retired them from its Glasgow-London service.

Sorting out the finances
On its first day in business, while still maintaining the previous frequencies and timings, new duty schedules gave Ulsterbus a 25% improvement in staff deployment – 1,200 staff against the previous requirement of 1,600 – and by the end of the financial year the accounts were showing a profit of £278,000.

During that summer, Heubeck told managers that the company needed to increase its surplus by £300,000 a year from additional revenue, services and private hire.

One of the first service developments around then was the introduction of a through Belfast-Cavan-Galway service, joint with CIÉ, its Republic of Ireland counterpart, a service which still runs in 2022. A Coleraine-Dublin service followed in 1971 (weekends only now), but opposition from the state-owned railways on both sides of the border delayed the introduction of a Belfast-Dublin service until 1989.

The first cross-channel service was introduced in 1970, between Glasgow and Londonderry via the Stranraer-Larne ferry, operated jointly with Western SMT. It was extended across Scotland to Edinburgh in 1977 and still runs today as part of the Scottish Citylink network.

Several others have been and gone. Belfast-Middlesbrough started in 1974. Sealink's withdrawal in 1975 of the ferry between Belfast and Heysham prompted the introduction of a seasonal Belfast-Blackpool service. Birmingham and London were reached from Belfast in 1976 in a joint operation with Western SMT and National Travel West. Manchester and Leeds were served from 1977, joint with National Travel East, while a weekend, overnight service between Belfast, Scarborough

and Filey began in 1978, worked entirely by Ulsterbus Tours vehicles. A Belfast-Cheltenham-Bristol service began in 1981, followed a few years later by Belfast-Leeds-Sheffield-Nottingham-Leicester.

Express services within the province were enhanced from 1979 with improved frequencies on routes linking Belfast with Enniskillen and Omagh and acceleration of others by diverting them on to motorways.

Local bus services were also improved, particularly offpeak.

ABOVE: Werner Heubeck was managing director of Ulsterbus from 1967 to 1988.

LEFT: Typical of the crew-operated vehicles that were a priority for Ulsterbus to replace was 944 (OZ 2131), a 1951 Leyland Titan PD2/10 with 59-seat lowbridge body built in the UTA's Belfast workshops. The Gallaher's cigarettes advertised on the side were manufactured in Ballymena. HOWARD CUNNINGHAM

Town services were introduced quickly at Omagh, Enniskillen and Newtownabbey while those at Carrickfergus and Larne were revised and enhanced in frequency. During 1971, Derry City services were revised to combat traffic congestion, town services were introduced in Antrim, the routes linking Coleraine, Portrush and Portstewart were revised to operate as a triangle and, in April that year, all services were renumbered, with limited stop and expresses put into the 200 series.

The north coast routes of Coastal Bus Service returned to state-owned operation with the takeover in April 1974 of that concern whose business had been badly affected by the downturn in tourism that followed the outbreak of the prolonged Troubles in 1969. Some services operated by Sureline Coaches were also taken over that year, allowing Ulsterbus to design better services for the developing new town of Craigavon; it took until June 1987 before the UTA services which had been taken over by Sureline in 1966 returned to state-owned operation.

A re-examination of town services in 1987/88 resulted in the introduction of minibuses at Bangor, Newtownards, Comber and Portrush. Minibuses also took over the service linking Belfast city centre and the International Airport at Aldergrove in 1988; today it requires double-deckers.

Ulsterbus has long maintained one depot on the British mainland, at Stranraer in Dumfries & Galloway, as a base for coaches operating into Scotland, England and Wales. In 1987, as an exercise in case privatisation or liberalisation of licensing was ever applied in Northern Ireland and also to provide year-round work at Stranraer, it tendered for, and won some contracts from Dumfries & Galloway Council for journeys on routes in the Newton Stewart area, which it branded as Macharsbus. These were services 302/303 to Whithorn via Port William and schooldays only service 301 journeys to Glentrool. This went down badly with SBG senior management – their displeasure was expressed at the highest levels – and Ulsterbus did not tender the next time round.

Belfast city services
Services within the Belfast city boundary had long been the sole preserve of the corporation's transport department, but new housing developments were

constructed outside the city limits in the 1960s, putting them firmly in UTA territory. However, corporation routes in the Glengormley area were extended to new estates in 1965, putting the transport department into a profit and leading it to seek extensions on other routes.

Ulsterbus management was suspicious of the UTA's calculations regarding route viability and was reluctant to hand over routes and revenue. The street violence, which erupted in 1969, focused management minds on more urgent matters, but there were some changes, such as Ulsterbus withdrawing its service to the Four Winds area and the corporation replacing it by extending its 37 route beyond its Ormeau terminus. Three Ulsterbus routes to housing estates in west Belfast, which were just beyond the boundary, transferred to the corporation in 1971/72, which helped stem losses caused by the "black taxi" paratransit operations in the area.

The question of who operated what and where in the boundary area was effectively resolved in April 1973 when the operations of the corporation transport department came under the control of the Northern Ireland Transport Holding Company (NITHC) in common management

with Ulsterbus. The new operation was named Citybus, though legal complications meant that the limited company did not come into existence for another two years. Heubeck was not keen to take over the loss-making corporation operation, but was given no choice.

One of the problems he identified was fare collection. To speed up boarding and reduce cash handling, Belfast Corporation had introduced a flat fare and payment by tokens in February 1970. It was open to abuse – passengers not inserting the correct number of tokens – and the company calculated in 1976 that it was losing at least £500,000 a year.

The situation was turned around into a £500,000 profit in

1977 and the token system was replaced in April 1978 with a multi-journey card system where passengers cancelled their own tickets; this was also open to fraud, thought to be costing 14% of revenue. Tickets were either just being used over and over, with some passengers applying candlewax so that the ink stamp could be wiped off at the end of a journey. In November 1988, responsibility for cancelling tickets reverted to drivers and revenue immediately increased not by the suggested 14%, but by 25%.

Citybus still exists today, but trades as Translink Metro. It now operates into some of those estates outside the city boundary, such as Ballybeen, Tullycarnet and

LEFT: Standard vehicle for many Ulsterbus services was the Leyland Leopard with Alexander body built in the Belfast area. This is 1922 (HOI 2922), new in 1975.

Rathcoole, which had been high
frequency Ulsterbus operations.

The price of the Troubles

No record of Northern Ireland
in the 1970s and 1980s would
be complete without mention
of the rioting, bombing and
shootings, which became known
as The Troubles. Ulsterbus
could not have taken over at
a more inopportune moment,
as the violence erupted from
1969, the first major attack on
company premises being at
Kilkeel, Co. Down on June 13/14
when a Bedford SB5, an Albion
Aberdonian, two Leyland Tiger
Cubs, three Leyland Royal Tigers
and a youthful Bedford VAM14
were destroyed.

As the years went on, there
were more incidents when

large numbers of vehicles were
destroyed in one night, such as at
Belfast (Smithfield) on June 12,
1978 when 21 were lost. Thirty
were destroyed at Londonderry
(Pennyburn) in two attacks in
February and December 1978, and
26 at Armagh on April 27, 1982.
Citybus lost 40 in February 1980
in attacks on its depots at Falls
Park (19 buses) and Ardoyne (21).

When the IRA attacked
Pennyburn on 19 February
1978 and destroyed 19 buses,
three were Bristol RELLs only
delivered in preceding days and
which may never have turned a
wheel in revenue-earning service.
Forty Leyland Atlanteans ordered
for delivery to Citybus between
August 1975 and March 1976
never all operated together,
one of them being hijacked and

destroyed after only three weeks
in service.

Mitigation for some of these
losses was to retain older vehicles
for longer than intended, but
that could not go on forever. Such
levels of destruction prompted
the acquisition of secondhand
vehicles, including AEC Merlins
and Swifts from London
Transport, London Country
and Mid-Warwickshire Motors,
Daimler Fleetline single-deckers
from Potteries and Northern
General, Leyland Leopards
from Grey-Green, Ribble and
Southdown and Bristol REs from
many sources.

Two other records of The
Troubles should also be made.
One was the murder by terrorists
of 12 members of staff – four of
them killed by a bomb at Oxford

Street bus station on 21 July 1972, a day since known as Bloody Friday when 22 bombs exploded in Belfast, including at Ulsterbus's three bus stations. The other is the action of the managing director in removing suspect and viable devices from buses; this was neither stupidity nor bravado, just instinct and experience.

Standard vehicle intake
Most vehicles that Ulsterbus inherited had bodies built in the UTA's workshops, an arrangement that ended with the formation of the new company. Many were only suitable for crew operation – Leyland Tiger PS1 single-deckers and Titan PD2 and PD3 double-deckers, some of which were to lowbridge layout — so it was a priority to ensure that

enough vehicles suitable for one-man-operation were available, hence the secondhand Leyland single-deckers.

In 1966, the government at Stormont allocated Ulsterbus a limited budget to purchase new vehicles, resulting in orders for six 10m Leyland Leopard/Plaxton Panorama coaches for touring and private hire, seven 11m Leopards with Alexander Y-type bodies built in Belfast by Potters for express services and 70 Duple (Northern)-bodied Bedford VAM14 buses with Leyland engines, Duple having promised delivery in time for the launch of the new company.

The front-engined Bedfords would not have been the first choice for new vehicles, but with the funding available for 70, that made a good show for the new company. The first arrived on March 12, 1967. They were used on all types of work – local service, express services, tours and private hire – to such an extent that they achieved twice the average mileage of Bedford-engined VAMs introduced by Eastern Scottish at the same time. This heavy use caused some engineering issues, which were quickly resolved, with several of the type running until 1979/80.

Fleet replacement began as soon as Ulsterbus was up and running, with tenders invited for 75 single-deckers vehicles for 1968 delivery, resulting in orders for ten Bristol LHs, 45 Leyland Leopards and 20 Bristol RELLs, all to be bodied by Potter of Belfast. In the event, the bodies on the RELLs were built by Alexander's Falkirk factory and in 1969 Alexander's acquired a majority shareholding in the Belfast coachbuilder, which over the next 20 years built the majority of bodies for Ulsterbus and Citybus. Those Leopards were a mix of 49- and 53-seaters, which with a standing capacity of up to 22 were able to replace the 59/60-seat crew-operated Titan PD2s.

The only double-deckers ordered at this time were 40 Leyland Atlanteans delivered between 1971 and 1973, with Alexander bodies built in Northern Ireland from parts supplied from Falkirk.

New single-deckers delivered in the 1970s and early 1980s included 681 Leyland Leopards, 260 Bristol RELLs, 100 Bristol LHs and 176 mid-engined Bedford YRTs, YRQs and YLQs (five of the YRQs and YLQs were Duple Dominant touring coaches).

It only had one Leyland National, supplied in 1972 in a failed attempt by Leyland to sell many more, but with Leyland intending to discontinue the Bristol RE, which it had kept in production almost exclusively for Ulsterbus and Citybus, it supplied the two fleets with trial batches of six B21 chassis (based on Leyland National running units) in 1981 and seven Lynx underframes in 1985, all bodied locally by Alexander. No orders resulted.

Ulsterbus graduated from the Leopard to the Tiger, starting in 1983 with two Duple Dominant IV coaches. Most had the bus chassis frame and Alexander N-type body in dual purpose, express coach or bus-seated form. The chassis was adapted for city use in Belfast, with a lower floor, Gardner engine and lower ratio axle. Double-deckers remained out of favour, though a small number of Atlanteans was kept at a few Ulsterbus depots for heavy schools traffic, these being supplemented by secondhand acquisitions.

Despite its difficult start and the relentless losses caused by the Troubles, the fleet was in sufficiently good shape for Ulsterbus to release some serviceable vehicles to the cross-border Lough Swilly company between 1976 and 1980. Leyland Tiger Cubs, although around 20 years old, were similar to that company's own buses purchased new in the late 1950s and still operating. Fourteen-year-old Leopards bought by the UTA or Ulsterbus as express coaches were a welcome addition. The Swilly was initially reluctant to take the other type on offer, some of the 1967 delivery of Bedford VAM14s, but took several when it came to realise how limited its options were.

Profits and premises

Ulsterbus was profitable from the start, achieving a surplus of £278,000 after its first ten months' trading and 20 years later, despite passenger numbers having fallen by about 25%, it recorded a profit of £3.9million, a surplus of almost 19%. A substantial surplus was still being recorded for Ulsterbus until the late 1990s, though things were not quite so good with Citybus, with profits generated in the 1970s turning to losses by the late 1980s.

Unlike Ulsterbus, Citybus faced fierce competition, particularly on its north and west Belfast routes, from unlicensed secondhand FX4 taxis operating as paratransit, more frequently than Citybus and often providing the only service when bus services were withdrawn during street disturbances.

In its early days, Ulsterbus continued to use former UTA garages and stations, but as these were now in the ownership of the NITHC, a rent had to be paid. It reduced the number of sites occupied and also opened new bus stations, built to a standard, functional design at Larne (November 1970), Bangor (October 1971), Enniskillen (1971), Downpatrick (January 1972), Newcastle (1979), Coleraine (1979) and Dungannon (December 1984).

Engineering facilities were also constructed at Larne,

Downpatrick, Enniskillen, Coleraine, Newry, Craigavon, Londonderry and also at Ballymena, which received new office accommodation and a new bus station across the yard from the railway station. These improvements were funded from the turnover and surplus earned by the company. However, ownership of some of the sites remained with the NITHC, though in recognition of the investment by Ulsterbus, it discontinued the rent, though took ownership of the new buildings.

Belfast never had a central bus station for city services. Most corporation and Citybus services departed from around the centrally located City Hall. Ulsterbus used three sites for its services, at Great Victoria Street, Oxford Street and Smithfield, the last mentioned being closed in September 1978 after a terrorist attack, with staff, vehicles and services transferring to Oxford Street and street stands nearby.

It was well into the 1980s before plans to redevelop the Great Victoria Street site were made, though these were complicated by the intention of Northern Ireland Railways to rebuild and reopen the line into the station it had closed in the mid-1970s. That site is currently being redeveloped as Belfast Grand Central station and is expected to open in 2025. It is not particularly central, however.

Expansion and possible privatisation

Werner Heubeck retired in 1988 to live in Shetland and died 21 years later. His successor, Ted Hesketh, who had been the company accountant, introduced more market research and promotion to relaunch the companies' image and services. Bus stations continued to be improved, with the basic designs of the 1970s replaced with modern Buscentres with significant architectural features.

Vehicle standards were upgraded, with seats added to the standee areas at Citybus, glassfibre seats replaced with cushioned squabs, new logos and typefaces were introduced, Citybus vehicles gaining a fleetname for the first time.

The express services of Ulsterbus were upgraded, starting in 1990 with 16 Alexander TE-bodied Leyland Tigers and the introduction of a new Goldline brand. Minibus services became Busybus. Both initiatives generated new business and increased passenger numbers, though these dropped again when the political situation improved after 1995.

The bus and railway companies were brought back under common management from 1996, as Translink. That effectively removed the possibility of privatisation, which had hung over the bus operations since the late 1980s. In case it was to leave the public sector, Hesketh and then chairman Bill Bradshaw developed a plan then for an employee buy-out led by the existing senior management team, but the security situation stopped it from proceeding.

The 1970s and 1980s were hard times in Northern Ireland, but the bus companies improved services, facilities and vehicles, and generated profits which were invested back into the business. It may well also have helped that the management teams were remarkably stable, with just two managing directors over the 36 years between 1967 and 2003. •